Men Around the Messenger

COMPANIONS OF THE PROPHET ﷺ SERIES

PART I

Men Around the Messenger

COMPANIONS OF THE PROPHET ﷺ SERIES

PART I

Khalid Muhammed Khalid

1 2 3 4 5 6 7 8 9 10

All rights reserved. No part of this publication may be reproduced, stored in a retrieval system or transmitted in any form or by any means – electronic, mechanical, photocopying, recording or otherwise – without written permission from the publisher.

© Light Publishing 2022

Khalid Muhammed Khalid

Men around the Messenger

Part I

ISBN 978-1-915570-05-5

www.lightpublishing.co.uk

بسم الله الرحمن الرحيم

CONTENTS

INTRODUCTION	9
MUHAMMAD ﷺ - THE LIGHT THEY FOLLOWED	11
MEN AROUND THE PROPHET	21
01 - Musab ibn Umair	21
02 - Salman Al-Farsi	31
03 - Abu Dhar Al-Ghifari	43
04 - Bilal ibn Rabah	59
05 - Abdullah ibn Umar	71
06 - Sa'ad ibn Abi Waqqas	83
07 - Suhaib ibn Sinan	95
08 - Muad ibn Jabal	101
09 - Al-Miqdad ibn Amr	109
10 - Sa'id ibn Amir	115
11 - Hamza ibn Abdul Muttalib	123
12 - Abdullah ibn Masud	137
13 - Hudhaifah ibn Al-Yamman	147
14 - Ammar ibn Yasir	157
15 - Ubadah ibn As-Samit	171
16 - Khabbab ibn Al-Arat	177
17 - Abu Ubaidah ibn Al-Jarrah	185
18 - Uthman ibn Madhuun	193
19 - Zaid ibn Haritha	201
20 - Jafar ibn Abu Talib	209

21 - Abdullah ibn Rawahah	219
22 - Khalid ibn Al-Walid	225
23 - Qais ibn Sa'ad ibn Ubadah	243
FAREWELL	249

INTRODUCTION

History recognises the great company of men that first followed in the footsteps of the Prophet Muhammad ﷺ. During the age of the Companions, all records required extraordinary attention to detail. And so, we are now left with a plethora of well-researched documentation about that period of Islamic history, and about the men around the Prophet ﷺ.

Successive generations of scholars have subjected even the smallest details of their lives to a great deal of scrutiny. These men's lives are not stuff of legend. These are facts characteristic of the personalities of the Prophet's own Companions. They are exalted and ennobled, not because of the author of their stories, but because of what the Companions themselves desired, and the immense effort they made to attain perfection.

They devoted their entire lives to the cause of Islam, offering personal sacrifice in their dedication to the Messenger ﷺ and to his call to faith. When the world was craving for someone to remove the shackles from a troubled humanity, these Companions stood by their great Messenger as pioneers.

One can only imagine how those righteous men achieved what they did in just a few years. How did they triumph over the ancient world, with all its empires and sovereignties? How did they build a new world with Allah's Quran and His Words? Above all, how were they able to illuminate human conscience with the truth of monotheism, forever sweeping away centuries of ancient paganism? This was their real miracle.

Of course, their achievements were simply a modest reflection of the greater miracle that was, and is, Allah's noble Quran. On the day that His honourable Messenger was commanded to deliver the message, Islam began to offer enlightenment to all.

In this book, we present 60 personalities of the Prophet's Companions, (may Allah have mercy upon them all). As mentioned at the conclusion of this book, these 60 men represent several thousand others of their brethren, who were contemporaneous with the Messenger ﷺ, and who also believed in and supported him. In their reflection we see the images of all the Companions. We recognise their faith, their constancy, their heroism and their loyalty to Allah and His Messenger ﷺ. And we will see here the effort they exerted, the calamities they endured, and the victory they achieved.

Now, let us discover more about these righteous men, to better understand the most graceful and virtuous of human examples. Let us see under their humble outer appearances, and discover the most sublime of people in greatness and wisdom. Let us appreciate their piety, and follow their stories as they spread the faith of Islam to liberate mankind.

Khalid Muhammad Khalid

MUHAMMAD ﷺ
THE LIGHT THEY FOLLOWED

Muhammad ibn Abdullah became Allah's Messenger ﷺ in the midsummer of his life. He was always filled with greatness and honesty, modesty and loyalty. He was devoted to the truth, and revered both life and the living. Allah's bounty towards him was great. He bestowed upon him the blessing of carrying His standard and speaking on His behalf.

It was Muhammad's rare eminence that secured his Companions' loyalty and made him a teacher and a friend to them. Companions such as Abu Bakr, Talhah, Az-Zubair, Uthman ibn Affan, Abdur Rahman ibn Awf, and Sa'ad ibn Abu Waqqas, *all* abandoned their wealth and glory in favour of Islam. With that choice came heavy burdens in life, and a great deal of conflict. But, still more hastened to his call.

What made those who believed in the Prophet ﷺ only increase in number? Though he declared day and night, "I hold no good or harm for you. I do not know what will become of me or you!" What then made them believe that the Quran they were reciting in secret, would one day reverberate in strong tones - not only in their own society, but throughout the ages, the world over? What made them believe the prophecy brought to them by the Messenger ﷺ? What filled their hearts with certainty and perseverance?

Of course, it was Muhammad ibn Abdullah himself.

They saw with their own eyes all his virtues and all that distinguished him. They saw his chastity, his purity, his honesty, his straightforwardness and his courage. They saw his eloquence and witnessed, first-hand, his daily revelations. These men watched Muhammad grow up and were his contemporaries throughout his life. His childhood was not limited to close relations, but instead witnessed by the people of Makkah as a whole. That was because his childhood was not like any other, it drew attention to itself for its early signs of maturity.

For example, the Quraysh used to talk about Abdul Muttalib's grandson who kept away from the children's playgrounds. And whenever he was invited to their celebrations, he would say, "I was not created for that." When his wet nurse, Halima, took him back to his people, she too told them about her observations, her experience with the child and what she saw in him to convince them that he was no ordinary boy. She believed there was a hidden secret in him, unknown except to Allah, which might be revealed one day.

———— •◦• ————

And so it was that Muhammad ﷺ had a transparent life, from cradle to grave. His every step, every word, every movement, every dream were the right of all people from the day he was born. It was as if Almighty Allah wished to highlight his reason and intellect through the transparency of his deeds.

If throughout a person's life you have only known them to be pure, truthful and honest, is it logical that such a person would suddenly start telling lies after the age of 40? Would he lie about Allah in order to claim he was His Messenger ﷺ, chosen and inspired by Him? Intuitively, no. This was the attitude of, not only the early believers, but also the Muhajirun (Emigrants) towards Allah's Messenger ﷺ, and indeed all those who sheltered him. They saw him not only sharing the trouble and hunger that befell people, but establishing for himself a core principle which was, "To be the first to feel hunger if people go hungry, and the last to satisfy [one's] hunger when people [are] starving." A man who had such an enlightened life could not play false with Allah. So, the believers saw the light of Allah, and they too began to follow Him.

Many unperceived blessings and spoils were bestowed upon the Companions, while the Prophet himself became more modest, more austere and more pious. Throughout his life, it was clear that such a man was not seeking wealth, money or sovereignty. When these were offered to him in recognition of his triumphant leadership, Muhammad ﷺ rejected them all. Till his last breath he devoted himself only to Allah - repentant and chaste.

He never deviated from the purpose of his great life, and never broke a promise to Allah in worship. No sooner would the latter part of the night begin, than he would get up, make his ablution and invoke Allah's name. Mountains of wealth and money were accumulated on his behalf, yet he never took more from it than the poorest of the Muslims would. He died leaving only his armour to bequeath.

Kings and countries received his invite to Islam with awe. But, not an atom of arrogance befell his character. When he saw people approaching him in nervous reverence, he said to them "Be easy, my mother used to eat dried meat in Makkah." Such was his humility.

When he conquered Makkah, the enemies of his faith put down their weapons and bowed their heads to await his judgment. But, he merely said, "Disperse, you are free!" Even at the height of the victory (to which he had devoted his life), he deprived himself of it. Instead, he walked in the victory procession on the Day of the Conquest with his head bowed. He repeated prayers of thanks to Allah in low tones, eyes wet with tears until he reached the Kaba. He then confronted the idols and said, "*Truth has come and falsehood has vanished, indeed, falsehood is bound to vanish.*" (17:81)

He was a man who spent his young life in purity and contemplation. After he received the revelation, he spent the remainder of his days in worship, guidance, and struggle. How could such a man be a liar? Surely, such a man and such a Messenger was above that. His Companions agreed.

We have mentioned that logic and reason were - and still are - the best proof of the truth for Muhammad ﷺ when he said, "I am Allah's Messenger." It does not appeal to good logic or to sound reason that a man who lived such a good life would lie about Allah. Early believers who hastened to believe in his message, and whom we are honoured to know something about through the pages of this book, believed in such logic. We see Muhammad ﷺ before his message and we see him after his message. We see him in his cradle and we see him near the grave. But, have we seen any contradiction or inconsistency in his life? Never.

Let us now approach the first years of his message. Those were the years that opened the living book of his life and heroism and, more than any other years, represented the cradle of his miracles. Throughout those years, the Messenger of Allah ﷺ was alone. He left all the possessions of comfortable, secure and settled life. He approached the people with what they were not familiar with, or rather with what they detested. He approached them and chose his words to appeal their reason, rather than emotions. It was a difficult task indeed, and so he approached it with an artfulness specific to him.

During Muhammad's time people worshipped idols, and their rites were observed as a religion. The Messenger ﷺ did not use the path of least resistance. It would have been easier for him to avoid direct confrontation, but he chose not to. This illustrates that he was indeed a Messenger. He heard a divine voice within him telling him to rise, and he did so willingly. He confronted his people in the plainest of terms, saying: "O people, I am the Messenger of Allah unto you, to worship Him and not to set partners with Him. These idols are intellectual falsehood. They are of no harm or benefit to you."

One might think that after this initial show of dedication, Muhammad ﷺ would worship his Lord as he liked, generally leaving the deities and his community's religion alone. If such a notion occurred to some Makkans at that time, the Prophet soon dispelled it. He made it quite clear that as a Messenger, he had a message to convey, and that he would not stay silent after receiving such guidance. In fact, nothing could have silenced him, because it was Allah who caused him to speak, and guided his footsteps.

The Quraysh's response was swift. One day, the noblemen of the Quraysh complained to Abu Talib: "Verily, we cannot tolerate a person who insults our fathers, mocks our dreams and finds fault with our deities. You either stop him, or we fight both of you until one of the parties is destroyed." Abu Talib sent a message to his nephew saying, "My nephew, your people have approached me and talked about your affairs. You have to think of me and yourself and not burden me with what I cannot endure."

The Messenger ﷺ did not hesitate and was resolute in his response: "O uncle, by Allah, if they put the sun on my right and the moon on my left in order to abandon this matter until it is manifested by Allah or I perish by it, I would never abandon it." Abu Talib thereupon restored his courage and the courage of his forefathers at once, clasped the right hand of his nephew with his two hands, and said, "Say what you like, for, by Allah, I will never force you to do anything at all."

From this point onwards, Muhammad ﷺ did not depend on his uncle for protection (though his uncle was capable of that) but he himself bestowed security, protection and steadfastness on the people around him. This inspired their love, loyalty, and belief in the Messenger ﷺ.

---·◊·---

His persistence regarding truth, his perseverance with the message and his patience during great troubles were all for the sake of Allah and not for any personal benefit. Such sacrifices were bound to attract the attention of brilliant minds, and those with good conscience. His Companions watched as harm reached the Prophet ﷺ from every corner. The solace he had sought in his uncle Abu Talib and his wife Khadija was also soon denied to him because they both died within days of each other.

The persecution became incredibly intense after this. One day for instance, the Messenger ﷺ went to the Kaba where the nobles of the Quraysh laid in wait for him as he performed his circumambulation. Suddenly, they surrounded him saying, "Is it you that says (such-and-such a thing) about our deities?" He calmly answered them "Yes, I say that." They held him by the ends of his clothes while Abu Bakr pleaded with them for his release: "Are you going to kill a man for saying, Allah is my Lord?"

As if the hostility from his own clan wasn't enough, the Prophet ﷺ was subjected to further abuse from those who were not related or known to him. But, Almighty Allah had commanded him to deliver the message, and so he did not falter. He would often remember a time when the intransigence of his community was so intense, that he returned home sorrowful, and huddled to cover himself in his bed. In that moment he heard the voice of revelation urging him to rise once more: *O You covered - Arise and warn.* (74:1-2)

So, he persisted in delivering Allah's message and warning against deviation. He did not care about harm befalling him, and he did not search for comfort. When he visited Taif to spread his message, the nobles of the community there were more cunning than their Makkan counterparts. Instead of abusing him themselves, they set their children and hooligans against him - abandoning the most sacred custom of the Arabs, that of hospitality to guests and the protection of one who seeks help.

Muhammad ﷺ escaped to a nearby orchard during the pursuit of the hooligans. His right hand was stretched towards heaven praying to Allah while his left protected his face from the stones being thrown at him. Even in such a stressful moment, the Prophet called to his Creator with courtesy and eloquence: "O Allah, to you I complain of the weakness of my strength, my inability to find a way, and my humiliation by the people. O the Most Compassionate, You are the Lord of the weak, and You are my Lord. To whom do You entrust me? To a distant relation who ignores me, or to an enemy who has power over me? If you are not angry with me, I do not care for other things, but granting me your mercy is too generous of you. I seek refuge in the light of Your face that brightens the darkness and amends the affairs of this world and the next. Do not be angry or dissatisfied with me. I beg your favour until You are satisfied with me. There is no strength or power except through You."

What loyalty the Prophet ﷺ had to his call to Islam! He was an unarmed person facing plots at every turn, and yet he persisted, staying steadfast to Allah. On his return from Taif, the Makkan people did not sense any despair in him. In fact, he became more optimistic and more dedicated. He decided to present himself to other local tribes, reaching out to them in their own districts. One day he went to Banu Kindah, another day Banu Hanifah, then to Banu Amir and so on, from one tribe to another. He said to them all, "I am the Messenger of Allah to you. He commands you to worship Allah and not to take partners with him, and to abandon what you worship of idols." When he visited nearby tribes, Abu Lahab would follow him and say to the people, "Do not believe him, for he is calling you to what is false."

People watched on as the Messenger of Allah sought other believers and helpers, but he was met only with ingratitude and enmity. He also refused any bargains and worldly gains in exchange for faith, and so he continued to struggle.

———•◊•———

People marvelled at Muhammad ﷺ, but few believed in him. Despite their low numbers, his fellow Muslims provided him with comfort and company. But then the Quraysh decided that each tribe should be in charge of teaching the believers amongst them a lesson. So, suddenly, a storm of persecution descended upon the Muslims. It was at this point that Muhammad ﷺ surprised the community by ordering all Muslims to emigrate to Abyssinia to seek sanctuary with the Christian king there.

The Prophet, however, decided to remain in Makkah to face the Quraysh's aggression. Why not emigrate with them and convey the word of Allah in another place? After all, Allah is the Lord of the worlds, not the Lord of the Quraysh alone. Furthermore, there were among the Muslims a good number of the noblest families of the Quraysh. Some of the most powerful tribes represented were Banu Umaiyah (Uthman ibn Affan, Amr ibn Sa'id ibn Al-As and Khalid ibn Sa'id ibn Al-As), Banu Asad (Az-Zubair ibn Al-Awam, Al-Aswad ibn Nawfal, Yazid ibn Zamah, and Amr ibn Umaiyah), and finally Banu Zahrah (Abdur Rahman ibn Awf, Amir ibn Abu Waqqas, Malik ibn Ahyab, and Al-Muttalib ibn Azhar). Many of the families of these Muslims would not stand their relatives' persecution for much longer. Why, then, did the Messenger ﷺ not let them stay with him to support him and to show his power?

Of course, he did not want a civil war, even if the probability of success weighed in his favour. But it was the Messenger's compassion above all that drove this decision. He could not bear to see his people being persecuted unnecessarily because of him. Of course, sacrifice could be made where there was no other choice, but when suffering was avoidable, it only made sense to send the Muslims to safety. But again, why not join them too? Simply, he was not commanded to. His place was to remain among the idols, to keep uttering Allah's name in their midst. He continued to be harmed for his beliefs, but he stayed steadfast and held true to his sacrifice.

The man and the Messenger manifested perfectly in Muhammad ﷺ. Those who doubted his message had no such doubts about his reputation, the purity of his character, or his humanity. Allah had chosen a man who was the best in both standing and honesty. The Prophet was heard reprimanding others if they ever exaggerated in glorifying him, or even sometimes when they simply over complimented him. If they were seated when he walked in a room, he prohibited them from standing up to honour him. He said, "Do not stand as non-Arabs do when they glorify one another."

When the sun eclipsed on the day of the death of his beloved son Ibrahim, the Muslims mentioned that the eclipse must have been a reflection of sadness for the loss of his son. But even in his state of mourning, the Messenger ﷺ hastened to refute this assumption before it became legend. He addressed them saying, "The sun and the moon are two of the signs of Allah. They never eclipse for the death or life of anybody."

Muhammad ﷺ was entrusted with the minds of his people, and so accomplishing his task and spreading Islam in the right way was crucial to him. He was certain that he came to humanity to change their way of life and that he was not a Messenger to the Quraysh, or even to the Arabs alone; but he was Allah's Messenger to all people on earth.

Almighty Allah directed his vision and the Prophet ﷺ perceived the truth of the faith he announced and the living immortality it would have. Nevertheless, he did not see himself or his unprecedented success as more than a brick in the construction. As he once said, "The relation between prophets who came before me and myself is like a man who built a house and constructed it well and decorated it, except for a brick in one of its corners. This made people go round it and express their astonishment, saying, will this brick not be put in place? I am such a brick and I am the last of the prophets."

All that long life he lived - all his struggles and heroism, his glory and purity, all the victory achieved after his death - all of this was nothing but a brick, a mere brick in a lofty and deep-rooted building. He was the one who proclaimed this and reiterated it. In addition, he did not make up such a speech out of assumed modesty, or to nourish a hunger for glory. He emphasised this brick analogy because it was fact and quintessential to his message.

That was the teacher of mankind and the last of the prophets. He was the light seen by the people, and he lived amongst them just as any other man. Then, after his departure from this world, he was seen by the whole world as a preserver of truth.

Now, while we meet a number of his noble Companions on the following pages of this book - where we will be astonished by their faith, their sacrifices, and the good cause they set their lives for – the reason for their marvellous lives will be clear before us.

This reason was nothing but the light they followed in Muhammad, the Messenger of Allah ﷺ. Almighty Allah combined in him the vision of truth and self-dignity, which illuminated the destiny of mankind.

(1)

MUSAB IBN UMAIR

The First Envoy of Islam

Musab was a gem amongst the Quraysh, he was handsome and youthful. Historians and narrators describe him as "the most charming of the Makkans". He was born and brought up in wealth and luxury. There was perhaps no boy in Makkah who was pampered more by his parents than Musab ibn Umair. This mirthful youth was the talk of the ladies of Makkah, the crown jewel of their gatherings – how was it possible for him to become one of the legends of the faith?

By Allah, the story of Musab ibn Umair (or 'Musab the Noble', as he was known among the Muslims) is an interesting tale. He was one of those 'made' by Islam, and fostered by the Prophet Muhammad ﷺ. As a young man, he too heard what the people of Makkah had begun to hear about Muhammad, the Truthful - that Allah had sent him as a bearer of glad tidings and a warner to call them to the worship of Allah, the one God. Whist in Makkah, Prophet Muhammad ﷺ and his religion was the talk of the town. And, this spoiled boy was one of the most attentive listeners.

That was because, although he was young, wisdom and common sense were among Musab's stronger traits. He heard that the Prophet ﷺ, and those who believed in him, were meeting far away from the dignitaries of Quraysh at As-Safa, in the house of Al-Arqam ('Dar Al-Arqam'). He wasted no time. He went one night to Dar Al-Arqam, yearning and anxious to know more. There, the Prophet was meeting with his Companions, and reciting the Quran.

As Musab heard the Prophet's recitation, a joy overwhelmed him and he came to Islam. The Prophet ﷺ patted Musab's throbbing heart with his blessed right hand. The young Musab already appeared to have more wisdom than his age and now he found an inner determination that would change the course of his lifetime.

Musab's mother was Khunas bint Malik, and people feared her almost to the point of terror because of her strong personality. When Musab became a Muslim, he was neither careful nor afraid of anyone on the face of the earth, except his mother. Even if Makkah, with all its idols and nobles were to challenge him, he would stand up to it. As for a dispute with his mother, this felt an impossible prospect, so he decided to keep his faith secret until such a time as Allah willed. In the meanwhile, he continued to frequent Dar Al-Arqam and take lessons from the Prophet ﷺ. He was satisfied with his faith and continued to avoid the wrath of his mother, who had no knowledge of his embracing Islam.

However, Makkah at that time kept no secret, for the eyes and ears of the Quraysh were everywhere, checking every footprint in the sand. Once, Uthman ibn Talha saw him carefully entering Al-Arqam's house, then he saw him another time praying like Muhammad ﷺ. No sooner had he seen him than he ran quickly with the news to Musab's mother, who was left astonished.

Musab stood before his mother, the people, and the nobles of Makkah there assembled, telling them the irrefutable truth. He recited the Quran with which the Prophet ﷺ had cleansed the Companions' hearts, filling them with honour, wisdom, justice, and piety. His mother wanted to punish him, but his recitation dulled her reaction, and together with this her maternal instinct spared him a beating. Instead though, she took him to a rough corner of her house and shut him in it. She put shackles on him and imprisoned him there until he heard the news of emigration of some believers to Abyssinia. He was able to delude his mother and his guards, to escape to Abyssinia.

Once there, he stayed in Abyssinia with his fellow emigrants, and then returned with them to Makkah when commanded. He also emigrated to Abyssinia for the second time with the Companions. But whether Musab was in Abyssinia or Makkah, the experience of his faith proclaimed itself in all places and at all times.

Musab became confident that his life was in service only to the Supreme Creator and his outward appearance soon reflected that too. One day, as he approached a group of Muslims, they lowered their heads and shed some tears on seeing him wear such worn out garments. They were accustomed to his former appearance before he had become a Muslim, when his clothes had been nothing but finery. The Prophet ﷺ however, held him with in high esteem and affection, he smiled and said "I saw Musab here, and there was no youth in Makkah more [pampered] by his parents than he. He then abandoned all that for the love of Allah and His Prophet!".

In the meanwhile, when she found that she could not bring him back to her religion, his mother withheld all his former luxuries from Musab. She refused to let anyone who had abandoned their gods to eat of her food, even if that meant her own son. Her last interaction with Musab was when she tried to imprison him for a second time after his return from Abyssinia. He swore that if she did that, he would kill all those who came to help her to lock him up. She knew the truth of his determination when he was intent on something, and so she simply bade him farewell.

The parting moment revealed a strange infidelity on the part of his mother, and a strong loyalty to faith on Musab's part. When she said to him, while turning him out of her house, "Go away, I am no longer your mother," he came close to her and said, "O mother, I am advising you and my heart is with you, please bear witness that there is no god but Allah and that Muhammad is His servant and Messenger." She replied to him, angrily, "By the stars, I will never enter your religion, to degrade my status and weaken my senses!"

And, so Musab left his mother and the great luxury in which he had been living behind. He became satisfied with a new, hard life; wearing the roughest of clothes, eating one day and going hungry another. This spirit, which was grounded in the strongest faith and adorned with the light of Allah, made him an entirely different man, one who appeals to the eyes of other great souls.

While he was in this state, the Prophet ﷺ commissioned him with the greatest task of his life, to be his envoy to Medina. His mission was to instruct the Ansar who believed in the Prophet and who had pledged their allegiance to him at Aqabah. He was also tasked with calling others to Islam, and with preparing Medina for the day of the great hijra. Among the Companions of the Prophet ﷺ there were others who were older, more prominent and nearer in relation to the Prophet than Musab. But Muhammad ﷺ chose Musab the Noble, knowing that he was entrusting to him the most important task of that time, putting Islam's fate in Medina in his hands. The radiant city of Medina was destined to be the home of hijra, and a springboard for Islamic enlightenment and saviours of the future.

Musab was equal to the task. He was equipped with an excellent mind and honourable character. He won the hearts of the Medinans with his piety, uprightness and sincerity. And so, they embraced the religion of Allah in droves. When the Prophet ﷺ first sent him there, only 12 Muslims had pledged allegiance to the Prophet during the first pledge of Aqabah. He had hardly completed a few months of his mission when they answered the call of Allah and the Prophet ﷺ. By the next pilgrimage season, the Medinan Muslims sent a delegation of 70 believing men and women to Makkah to meet the Prophet ﷺ.

This delegation came with their teacher and the Prophet's trusted envoy, Musab ibn Umair. Musab had proven, by his good sense and excellence, that the Prophet ﷺ knew well how to choose his envoys and teachers. He had understood his mission well. Musab knew that he was a caller to Allah and preacher of His religion, he was there to call people to right guidance and the straight path. Like the Prophet ﷺ in whom he believed, Musab was no more than a deliverer of the message. There he stood fast, with Asad ibn Zorarah as his host, and both of them would visit the local tribes, dwellings, and assemblies. There, they would recite to the people what had been revealed from the Book of Allah, and instil in them that Allah was no more than One God.

Musab and his companions encountered violence, and even near death experiences, on their mission, but he used his intelligence to overcome his adversaries. One day, for instance, he was taken by surprise while preaching in Medina by Usaid ibn Hudair, leader of the Abd Al-Ashhal tribe, who confronted him with a drawn arrow in his bow. He was raging with anger against the one who had come to corrupt the religion of his people by telling them to abandon their gods in favour of the unknown One God. Their gods were the centre of their worship and, they believed, their source of help in times of need.

As for the God of Muhammad, to whom this envoy was calling, nobody knew His place, nor could anybody see Him! When the Muslims who were sitting around Musab saw Usaid ibn Hudair advancing with his unbridled anger, they became frightened. But, Musab the Noble stood firm. Usaid stood before him and Asad ibn Zorarah shouted, "What brings you here? Are you coming to corrupt our faith? Go away if you wish to be saved!"

With the calmness and force of the sea, Musab eloquently said, "Won't you sit down and listen? If you like our cause, you can accept; and if you dislike it, we will spare you of what you hate." Usaid was a thoughtful and clever man, and here he saw Musab inviting him to listen and no more. If he was convinced, he would accept it; and if not, then Musab would leave his clan alone, and move to another neighbourhood without any harm involved. There and then Usaid answered him saying, "Well, that is fair," and dropping his arrow to the ground, he sat and listened.

Musab had hardly read the Quran, to explain the Prophet's mission, when the conscience of Usaid began to brighten and change through Allah's words. He became overwhelmed by their beauty. When Musab finished speaking, Usaid exclaimed to him and those with him "How beautiful is this speech and how true! How can one enter this religion?" Musab told him to purify his body and clothes and say, "I bear witness that there is no god but Allah." Usaid brought clean water to pour on his head, then proclaimed, "I bear witness that there is no god but Allah, and that Muhammad is the Messenger of Allah."

The news of his conversion spread like wildfire, so Sa'ad ibn Muad came next, to listen to Musab, and he too was convinced to embrace Islam. Next, came Sa'ad ibn Ubadah, and with these conversions a further blessing ensued. The people of Medina soon came together asking one another, "If Usaid ibn Hudair, Sa'ad ibn Muad and Sa'ad ibn Ubadah have embraced Islam, what are we waiting for? Go straight to Musab and believe. By Allah, he is calling us to the truth and the straight path!"

And so, the first envoy of the Prophet ﷺ succeeded beyond compare. It was a success which Musab fully deserved and to which he was equal.

The days and years passed by. The Prophet ﷺ and his Companions emigrated to Medina, and the Quraysh were raging in envious pursuit of the pious worshippers. The Battle of Badr soon took place, where the Quraysh were taught a lesson in the loss of their stronghold. So, they began preparing themselves for revenge – this took the form at the Battle of Uhud. The Muslims mobilised themselves, and the Prophet ﷺ stood in their midst to choose one of his faithful Companions to bear the standard during the battle. He called for Musab the Noble, to carry the standard.

As the battle raged, the fighting became more furious. Then, unfortunately, the rank of archers disobeyed the orders of the Prophet ﷺ by leaving their mountain top positions when they saw the Quraysh withdrawing. Sadly, this act soon turned the victory of the Muslims into a defeat. The Muslims were taken unaware by the cavalry of the Quraysh at the mountain top, and many Muslims were killed as a consequence.

When they saw the confusion and horror splitting the ranks of the Muslims, the polytheists concentrated on finishing off the Prophet of Allah ﷺ. Musab saw the impending threat, so he raised the standard high, shouting, "Allahu Akbar! (Allah is the Greatest!)" with the roar like that of a lion. He turned left and jumped right, fighting and killing the foe. All he wanted was to draw the attention of the enemy to himself in order to turn their attention away from the Prophet ﷺ. But his distraction technique was ebbing as the enemies multiplied around him.

Let us allow a witness to describe for us the last scene of Musab the Noble. Ibn Sa'ad narrates that Ibrahim ibn Muhammad ibn Sharhabul Al-Abdri related from his father, who said: "Musab ibn Umair carried the standard on the Day of Uhud. When the Muslims were scattered, he stood fast until he met Ibn Qumah who was a knight. He struck him on his right hand and cut it off, but Musab said, '...*and Muhammad is but a Messenger. Messengers have passed away before him*' (3:144). He carried the standard with his left hand and leaned on it. This time Ibn Qumah struck his left hand and cut it off, and so he leaned on the standard and held it with his upper arms to his chest, all the while saying, '...*and Muhammad is but a Messenger. Messengers have passed away before him*'. Then a third one struck him with his spear, and the spear went through him. Musab fell and so too did the standard."

The height of martyrdom had fallen. He fell after he had struggled for the sake of Allah in the great battle of sacrifice and faith. He had thought that if he fell, the Prophet ﷺ would be next, as he was without defence and protection. And so, he put himself in harm's way for the sake of the Prophet ﷺ. Overpowered by his fear for and love of him, he continued to say with every sword stroke that fell on him from the foe, ...*and Muhammad is but a Messenger. Messengers have passed away before him*. This verse was actually revealed only later, after Musab had spoken these words.

After the bitter battle, they found the body of the martyred Musab lying with his face in the dust, as if he feared to watch while harm befell the

Prophet ﷺ. When he fell as a martyr, he made sure of the safety of the Prophet of Allah, serving, guarding and protecting him to the very end.

The Prophet ﷺ and his Companions came to inspect the scene of the battle and bid farewell to its martyrs. Pausing at Musab's body, many tears fell from the Prophet's eyes. Khabbab ibn Al-Arat narrated: "We emigrated with the Prophet ﷺ for Allah's cause, so our reward became due with Allah. Some of us passed away without enjoying anything in this life and its reward, and one of them was Musab ibn Umair, who was martyred on the Day of Uhud. He did not leave behind anything except a sheet of shredded woollen cloth. If we covered his head with it, his feet were uncovered, and if we covered his feet with it, his head was uncovered. The Prophet ﷺ said to us, 'Cover his head with it and put grass over his feet.'"

The Prophet ﷺ suffered the loss of his uncle Hamza during the same battle, where his corpse was mutilated in such a way that it drew tears from the Prophet. Despite the terrible pain in his heart; despite the fact that the battlefield was littered with the corpses of his Companions (all of whom represented the peak of truth, piety and enlightenment); despite all this, he stood at the corpse of his first envoy, Musab, bidding him farewell and weeping bitterly. In fact, the Prophet ﷺ stood in tears by the remains of Musab ibn Umair saying, *"Among the believers are men who have been true to their covenant with Allah."* (33:23)

Then he gave a sad look at the garment in which he was shrouded and said, "I saw you in Makkah, and there was no one more precious, nor more distinguished one than you, and here you are bare-headed in a garment!" Then the Prophet ﷺ looked at all the martyrs in the battlefield and said, "The Prophet of Allah witnesses that you are martyrs to Allah on the Day of Resurrection." Then he gathered his living Companions around him and said, "O people, visit them, come to them, and salute them. By Allah, no Muslim will salute them but that they will salute him in return."

Peace be on you, O Musab. Peace be on you, O martyrs. Peace and blessings of Allah be upon you all.

(2)

SALMAN AL-FARSI

The Seeker of Truth

This time our hero hails from Persia, indeed in later years many from that region came to embrace Islam. Some of those Muslims were unsurpassable in both their faith, and their knowledge of religion and worldly affairs. Indeed, from all over the world, Islam birthed Muslim philosophers, physicians, jurists, astronomers, inventors, and mathematicians. They came from various nations, but their religion remained one.

The Prophet ﷺ had prophesied this blessed spread of his religion. Indeed, he had been so promised by his Almighty Lord. He had pointed to the time, place, and day, and he had seen in his vision the banner of Islam fluttering in all corners of the earth and over the palaces of its earthly rulers. Salman Al-Farsi ('the Persian') bore witness to this and was, in fact, firmly connected with what happened.

It was the Day of Al-Khandaq (The Trench) in the year 5 AH, when the leaders of the Jews approached Makkah to form an alliance against the Prophet ﷺ and the Muslims. They asked the polytheists there to form a treaty and enter into a decisive battle to eradicate this new religion. The war was planned. The Quraysh army and its allies would attack Medina from the outside, while the Banu Quraidhah would attack them from within. They would come from behind the ranks of the Muslims, to crush them from inside out.

And so, one day, the Prophet ﷺ and the Muslims were taken unaware by an enormous, well-armed army marching on Medina. The Quran depicts the scene thus: *When they came against you from above you and from below you, and your eyes turned away and your hearts reached to your throats, and you imagined vain thoughts about God; in that place the believers were tried and shaken most severely.* (33:10-11)

Under the command of Abu Sufyan and Uyainah ibn Hisn, 24,000 fighters were advancing on Medina to storm and lay siege to it. Their aim was to rid themselves of Muhammad, his religion, and his Companions once and for all. This hybrid army was an alliance of all the tribes who had common interests that were threatened by Islam. It was a last and decisive attempt embarked on by all the enemies of the Prophet ﷺ, based upon individual, collective, and tribal concerns.

The Muslims found themselves in a precarious situation. The Prophet ﷺ assembled his Companions for consultation. They were gathered to reach a decision on defence and battle, but how could they even put up a defence? Just then, a tall man with flowing hair, Salman Al-Farsi (for whom the Prophet ﷺ bore great respect), raised his head and looked at Medina. The city was surrounded by hills and exposed open country, which could be easily broken in to by the enemy.

Salman had much experience in warfare and its tactics in his native Persia. So, he proposed to the Prophet ﷺ something which the Arabs had never seen before in battle. It was the digging of a trench in the exposed places around Medina. Allah only knows what could have become of the Muslims in that battle had they not dug that trench. It was no sooner seen by the Quraysh than they were stunned into despair. The forces of the enemy still remained in their tents for a month, unable to take Medina, until Allah sent them a storm one night which devastated their tents and tore them asunder. Then Abu Sufyan announced to his forces that they should return to where they had come from. They were despondent and frustrated.

During the excavation of the trench, Salman took his place among the Muslims as they dug and removed the sand. The Prophet himself was also taking part in digging with Salman's group. Their pickaxes could not smash a stubborn rock, in spite of the fact that Salman was of strong build. A single stroke of his would normally break a rock to pieces, but he stood in front of this stubborn one. He let all those around him try to break it, but in vain. Salman went to the Prophet ﷺ to ask him to divert the trench around that stubborn and challenging rock.

The Prophet returned with Salman to see the rock himself. When he saw it, he called for a pickaxe and asked the Companions to keep back from the splinters. He said, "In the name of Allah," and then raised his blessed, firm hands gripping the pickaxe and let it fall. The rock cracked, letting out a great shaft of light. Salman said that he himself saw that light shining upon Medina. The Prophet ﷺ raised the pickaxe and gave a second blow and the rock broke further. At that moment the Prophet said loudly, "Allahu Akbar (Allah is the Greatest) I have been given the keys to Rome; its red palaces have been lit for me and my nation has vanquished it."

The Prophet ﷺ struck a third blow. The rock shattered with a blinding light. The Prophet told them that he was now seeing the palaces of Syria, Sana and others like them, the world over, where the banner of Islam would flutter one day. The Muslims shouted in deep faith, "This is what Allah and His Prophet have promised us!"

Salman was the originator of the project to dig the trench, and he was associated with the rock out of which poured some secrets of the unseen and of destiny. When he called the Prophet ﷺ to break it, he stood by his side, saw the light himself, and heard the glad omen. In fact, he lived to see the prophecy fulfilled and abided in its living reality. He saw the great capitals of Persia and Rome (Byzantium), the palaces of Sana, Syria, Egypt, and Iraq.

Here below, we have a first-hand account from Salman Al-Farsi, as he sits in the shade of a tree by his house in Medina, telling guests about his great adventures in the quest for truth. He explains to them how he abandoned the religion of his Persian people for Christianity and then for Islam. How he abandoned his father's wealth and estate and threw himself into the arms of the wilderness in the quest for the release of his tension and his soul. How he was sold in a slave market on his way to search for truth. And, how he finally met with the Prophet ﷺ and how he came to believe in him. Now let us listen to his grand tale from the Companion himself.

———•◊•———

I come from Isfahan, from a place called Jai. I was the most beloved son of my father, who was a figure of high esteem among his people. We used to worship fire. I devoted myself to the worship of fire until I became custodian of the fire which we lit and never allowed it to be extinguished.

My father had an estate. One day, he sent me there. I passed by a Christian church and heard them praying. I went in and saw what they were doing. I was impressed by what I saw in their prayers. I said, "This is better than our religion." I did not leave them until sunset nor did I go to my father's estate, nor did I return to my father until he sent people in search of me.

I asked the Christians about their prayers, which impressed me, and about the origin of their religion. They answered, "In Syria." I said to my father when I returned to him, "I passed by people praying in a church of theirs, and I was impressed by their prayer, and I could see that their religion is better than ours." He questioned me and I questioned him, and then he put fetters on my feet and locked me up.

Then I sent [word] to the Christians saying I had entered their religion, and I requested that whenever a caravan came from Syria, they should tell me before its return in order for me to travel with them - and so they did.

I broke loose from the iron fetters and I escaped. I set out with them for Syria. While I was there, I asked about their learned man, and I was told that he was the bishop - leader of the church. I went to him and told him my story. I lived with him, serving, praying, and learning. But this bishop was not faithful in his religion, because he used to gather money from the people to distribute it, but he would keep it for himself. Then he died.

They appointed a new leader in his place. I have never seen a man more godly than he in his religion, nor more active in his bid for the Hereafter; nor more pious in the world, nor more punctual at worship. I loved him more than I had ever loved any other person before. When his fate came, I asked him, "To whom would you recommend me? And to whom would you leave me?" He said, "O my son, I do not know anyone who is on the path that I am on and who leads the kind of life I lead, except a certain man in Mosul."

When he died, I went to that man in Mosul, and told him the story, and I stayed with him as long as Allah wished me to stay. Then death approached him [too]. So, I asked him, "To whom would you advise me to go to?" He directed me to a pious man in Nisibin." So, I went to him and told him my story. I stayed with him as long as Allah wished me to stay. When death overtook him, I asked him as before. He told me to meet a person at Amuriah in Byzantium. So, to Byzantium I went and stayed with that man, earning my living there by rearing cattle and sheep.

Then death approached him [as well], and I asked him, "To whom should I go?" He said, "O my son, I know no one anywhere who is on the path we have been on so that I can tell you to go to him. But you have been overtaken by an epoch in which there will appear a prophet in the pure creed of Ibrahim. He will migrate to the place of palm trees. If you can be sincere to him, then do so. He has signs which will be manifested: he does not eat of charity, yet he accepts gifts, and between his shoulders is the seal of prophethood. When you see him, you will know him."

A caravan passed by me on that day. I asked them where they had come from and learned that they were from the Arabian Peninsula. So, I told them, "I give you these cattle and sheep of mine in return for your taking me to your land." They agreed. So, they took me in their company until they brought me to Wadi Al-Qura, and there they wronged me. They sold me to a Jew. I saw many palm trees and cherished the hope that it was the land that had been described to me and which would be the future place of the advent of the prophet, but it was not.

I stayed with this Jew until another from Banu Quraidhah came to him one day and bought me from him. I stayed with him until we came to Medina. By Allah, I had hardly seen it when I knew that it was the land described to me.

I stayed with the Jew, working for him on his plantation in Banu Quraidhah until Allah sent His Prophet, who later emigrated to Medina and dismounted at Quba among the Banu Amr ibn Awf. Indeed, one day, I was at the top of a palm tree with my master sitting below it when a Jewish man came. He was a cousin of his and said to him, "May Allah destroy Banu Quba. They are spreading a rumour about a man at Quba who came from Makkah claiming that he is a prophet." By Allah, he had hardly said it, when I was seized by a tremor, and the palm tree shook until I almost fell on my master. I climbed down quickly saying, "What are you saying? What news?" My master gave me a nasty slap and said, "What have you got to do with this? Return to your work!"

So, I returned to work. At nightfall I gathered what I had and went out until I came upon the Prophet ﷺ at Quba. I entered and found him sitting with some of his Companions. Then I said, "You are in need and a stranger. I have some food which I intend to give out as charity. When they showed me your lodgings, I thought you most deserve it, so I have come to you with it." I put the food down. The Prophet ﷺ said to his Companions, "Eat in the name of Allah." He abstained and never took of it. I said to myself, "This, by Allah, is one sign. He does not eat of charity!"

I returned to meet the Prophet ﷺ again the next day, carrying some food, and said to him, "I can see that you do not partake of charity. I have something which I want to give to you as a present." I placed it before him. He said to his Companions, "Eat in the name of Allah" and he ate with them. So, I said to myself, "This indeed is the second sign. He eats of presents." I returned and stayed away for a while. Then I came to him, and I saw him sitting, having returned from a burial, and surrounded by his Companions. He had two garments, carrying one on his shoulder and wearing the other. I greeted him, then bent to see the upper part of his back. He knew what I was looking for, so he threw aside his garment off his shoulder and, behold, the sign between his shoulders, the seal of Prophethood, *was clear just as the Christian monk had described.*

At once, I staggered towards him, kissing him and weeping. He called to me to come forward and I sat before him. I told him my story as you have already heard me describe the events. When I became a Muslim, slavery prevented me from taking part in the battles of Badr and Uhud. Therefore, the Prophet ﷺ advised me, "Go into terms with your master for him to free you," and so I did. The Prophet told the Companions to assist me, and Allah freed me from bondage. I became a free Muslim, taking part with the Prophet ﷺ in the Battle of Khandaq and others.

With these simple words, Salman spoke of his noble and sacrificial adventure. Throughout his life he sought true religion, and finally found Islam. And it was Allah's guidance that helped Salman find his place in the world.

Salman achieved greatness through his restless spirit; a spirit that withstood difficulties and defeated them. He showed an unrelenting devotion to the truth. That sincerity led him voluntarily away from the estate of his father (with all its wealth and luxury) to the wilderness (with its difficulties and suffering). He moved from land to land, town to town. He sought new acquaintances, worshipped, persevered and searched for his destiny among varied people, sects, and different ways of life. Throughout all this, he adhered to the truth for the sake of guidance, until he was sold into slavery. After this, he was rewarded by Allah with the best of rewards - He brought Salman to the truth and brought him into the presence of His Prophet ﷺ. And Allah went on to grant him a long life, long enough for him to see the banner of Islam fluttering in all parts of the world.

Salman's character was one of nobility and truth and he lived a God-fearing life. In terms of the company he kept, he was the person nearest to Umar ibn Al-Khattab, and his piety was clear from the time he spent at Abu Ad-Darda's home. Abu Ad-Darda was known to pray all night and fast all day. Salman actually reprimanded him for this excessive worship. One day, he decided to stop him from fasting, explaining that it was supererogatory. Abu Ad-Darda asked him, "Would you prevent me from fasting for my Lord and from praying to Him?" Salman replied, "No, [but] your eyes have a claim over you, your family has a claim over you; so fast intermittently, then pray and sleep." Salman's advice reached the Prophet ﷺ who said, "Salman is, indeed, full of knowledge."

The Prophet ﷺ was often impressed by Salman's wisdom and knowledge, just as he was impressed by his character and religion. On the Day of Al-Khandaq the Ansar stood up and said, "Salman is of us," the Muhajirun stood up also and said, "Salman is of us." The Prophet responded to them too saying, "Salman is of us, O People of the House (Prophet's house)." Indeed, he deserved this honour!

He was held in the minds of Prophet's Companions with the highest regard and in the greatest position and respect. Ali ibn Abu Talib nicknamed him 'Luqman the Wise'. When asked about Salman after his death, Ali said, "Who among you is like Luqman the Wise? He was a man of knowledge who absorbed all the scriptures of the People of the Book. He was like a sea that was never exhausted!" Also, during the Caliphate of Umar, he came to Medina on a visit and Umar accorded him what he had never accorded to anyone before when he assembled his Companions and said, "Come, let us go out and welcome Salman!" They went on to receive him at the border of Medina.

After meeting him, Salman lived alongside the Prophet ﷺ, and after becoming a free Muslim, he would always worship with him too. He lived through the caliphates of Abu Bakr, Umar and, finally, Uthman - in whose era he met his Lord. Throughout these years, Islam began to spread everywhere, and the treasures of Islam were carried back to Medina. These treasures were then distributed to the people in the form of regular allowance and fixed salaries. Consequently, the responsibilities of governance increased on all fronts. So, where did Salman stand in this respect?

———◦◦———

Open your eyes. Do you see that humble man sitting there in the shade making baskets and utensils out of palm fronds? That is Salman. Take a good look at him. Look at his modest garment, which is so short that it only sits at his knees. That was Salman in his old age. He received a grant of 4,000 to 6,000 dirhams a year, but he distributed all of it, refusing to take a dirham. He used to say, "I would buy palm fronds with one dirham to work on and then sell it for three dirhams. I retained one dirham of it as capital, spent one dirham on my family, and gave away one dirham, and if Umar ibn Al-Khattab prevented me from that, I would not stop."

It is often presumed that the piety of the Companions (such as Abu Bakr, Umar, Abu Dhar and so on) was influenced by the general life of the Arabian Peninsula, where the Arabs found pleasure in simplicity. And yet, here we are with a Persian man, from the land of pleasure, luxury, and civilisation. He was not poor, but from the upper class of his society. And now he was refusing property, wealth, and enjoyment; insisting that he live on one dirham a day from the work of his hands?

Salman was known to refuse positions of authority, unless related to battle (and only if no one else was suitable for it, and it was forced upon him) - even then he would accept it with shyness. When he finally accepted leadership, which was also forced upon him, he refused to take his lawful dues. Hisham ibn Hasan relates from Hassan that: "The allowance of Salman was 5,000. He lived among 30,000 people and used to dress in a garment cut into halves. He wore one and sat on the other half. Whenever his allowance was due him, he distributed it to the needy and lived on the earnings of his hands."

Why do you think he was doing all this work and worshiping with such devotion? You can hear his own reply. While he was on his deathbed, readying to meet his Lord, Sa'ad ibn Abi Waqqas went to greet him, and Salman wept! Sa'ad said, "What makes you weep, O Abu Abdullah? The Prophet of Allah died pleased with you!" Salman replied, "By Allah, I am not weeping in fear of death, nor for love of the world. But the Prophet of Allah put me on an oath. He said, 'Let any of you have in this world like the provision of the traveller,' and here I have owned many things around me." Sa'ad said: "I looked around, and I saw nothing but a water-pot and vessel to eat in! Then I said to him, 'O Abu Abdullah, give us a parting word of advice for us to follow.' He said, 'O Sa'ad, remember Allah for your carers, if you have any. Remember Allah in your judgment, if you judge. Remember Allah when you distribute the share.'

This was the man who filled his spirit with riches just as it filled him with renunciation of the pleasures of this world. The oath which he and the rest of the Companions had taken before the Prophet of Allah was that they must not let the world possess them, and that they should take nothing from it but the provision of the traveller in his bag.

Salman had truly kept that oath, yet his tears still ran when he saw his soul preparing for departure, fearing that he had transgressed limits. There was barely anything around him when he passed, and yet still he considered himself lavish!

During the days of Umar's rule over Medina, Salman never changed his way. He had refused, as we have seen, to receive his salary as a leader, and simply went on weaving baskets to earn a living. His dress was no more than a gown, resembling his old clothes in simplicity.

One day while on the road, Salman met a man arriving from Syria, carrying a load of figs and dates. The load was too heavy for him and made him weary. No sooner did the Syrian see the man in front of him (who appeared to be a commoner and a poor person) he thought of putting the load on his shoulders, and in return he would give him something for his labour when he reached his destination. So, he beckoned to the man (Salman, the governor), and he came up to him. The Syrian said to him, "Relieve me of this load." He carried it, and they walked together.

While on their way, they met a group of people. He greeted them and they stood up in reverence, replying, "And unto the governor be peace!" "Who is the governor?" The Syrian asked himself. His surprise increased when he saw some of them rushing towards Salman to take the load off his shoulders. "Let us carry it, O governor". When the Syrian knew that he was the governor of Medina, he was astonished. Words of apology and regret tumbled from his lips, and he went forward to grab the load. But Salman shook his head in refusal, saying, "No, not until I take you to your destination."

He was asked one day, "What troubles you in leadership?" He replied, "The pleasure of nurturing it and the bitterness of meaning!"

A friend of his came to him one day at his house and found him kneading dough. He asked him, "Where is your servant?" He replied, "We have sent her on an errand and we hate to charge her with two duties." When we say 'his house' let us remember what kind of house it was.

When Salman thought of building it, he asked the mason, "How are you going to build it?" The mason was courteous and yet witty. He knew the piety and devotion of Salman, so he replied to him saying, "Fear not. It is a house for you to protect yourself against the heat of the sun and dwell in the cold weather. When you stand erect in it, it touches your head." Salman said to him, "Yes, that is it, so go on and build it."

There was nothing of the goods of this world which could attract Salman for a moment, nor did they leave any traces in his heart except one thing, which he was particularly mindful of and had entrusted to his wife, requesting her to keep it far away in a safe place. In his last sickness, and in the morning on which he gave up his soul, he called her, "Bring me the trust which I left in safe keeping!" She brought it and, behold, it was a bottle of musk. He had gained it on the day of liberating the city of Jalwala and kept it to be his perfume on the day of his death. Then he called for a pot of water, sprinkled the musk into it, stirred it with his hand and then said to his wife, "Sprinkle it on me, for there will now come to me creatures from the creatures of Allah. They do not eat food and what they like is perfume."

Having done so, he said to her, "Shut the door and go down." She did what he bade her to do. After a while she went up to him and saw his blessed soul had departed his body. It was gone to the Supreme Master, and it ascended with the desire to meet Him as he had an appointment there with the Prophet Muhammad ﷺ, and his two Companions Abu Bakr and Umar - the noble circle of martyrs!

Long had the burning desire stirred Salman. The time had come for him to rest in peace.

(3)

ABU DHAR AL-GHIFARI

An Enemy of Wealth

With great eagerness, Abu Dhar journeyed towards Makkah. The difficulty of his journey and the burning desert sand had made him suffer. But the goal he was striving for made him forget his pain altogether, he was in search of Muhammad ﷺ. He entered Makkah disguised as a pilgrim for the idols of the Kaba, because if the Makkans knew that he had come to listen to the Prophet ﷺ, they would not have let him leave alive. He did not fear this, but vowed that it would not happen before meeting the Messenger, because he believed in him and was convinced in the truth of his message.

He went about secretly gathering information and whenever he heard someone speaking about Muhammad ﷺ, he carefully approached them. He was able to compile scattered pieces of information which he had heard here and there, and finally he was guided to a place where he was able to meet him.

One morning he went there and found the Prophet ﷺ sitting alone. He approached him and said, "O my Arab brother, good morning." Thereupon the Prophet replied, "And may peace be upon you, my brother." Abu Dhar then said, "Sing to me some of what you are saying." The Prophet ﷺ answered, "It isn't a poem to be sung, but the Holy Quran." Abu Dhar said, "Then recite for me."

The Prophet recited to him while he listened. It was not long until Abu Dhar proclaimed, "I bear witness that there is no god but Allah, and that Muhammad is His Prophet and Messenger." The Prophet ﷺ asked him, "Where are you from, my Arab brother?" Abu Dhar answered, "From Ghifar." A broad smile appeared on the Prophet's lips and his face was filled with astonishment.

Abu Dhar was also smiling, for he knew well that the reason behind the Prophet's astonishment. It was because of his tribe. Ghifar was a tribe with a notorious reputation for highway robbery. Its people were famous for theft and were known as allies of darkness and night. Was it possible that one of them would embrace Islam while it was still a new, secret religion?

Narrating the story himself, Abu Dhar said: The Prophet ﷺ lifted his eyes out of astonishment, due to Ghifar's reputation. Then he said, "Allah guides whom He wills." Indeed, Allah guides whom He wills. Abu Dhar (may Allah be pleased with him) was one of those whom Allah wanted to be rightly guided and for whom He wanted the best.

His insight was always directed towards truth.

It has been narrated that he worshiped Allah during the period of jahiliyya, which means that he revolted against the worship of idols and turned towards the belief in One Great Creator. This means that Abu Dhar had hardly heard about the appearance of a prophet rejecting idols and calling to the worship of Allah, when he immediately set out and hastened to meet this new Messenger of Allah ﷺ.

Immediately, and without hesitation, Abu Dhar embraced Islam. His order among the converts was fifth or sixth, which means that he converted during the very earliest days of Islam. When he embraced Islam the Prophet ﷺ was still secretly whispering the call to Islam to himself and to the five others who believed in his message. Abu Dhar could not do anything except carry his faith within his heart, secretly leaving Makkah and returning to his people.

However, Abu Dhar – whose actual name was Jundub ibn Janadah – had a restless and agitated temper. He had been created with the innate desire to rebel against falsehood wherever he found it. He saw the idols around him as falsehood. Abu Dhar acknowledged the Prophet's preference to keep a lower profile for Islam at this stage, but he longed for the Muslims to shout the message aloud before his departure. So, immediately after embracing Islam, he turned to the Prophet ﷺ with the following question: "O Messenger of Allah, what is it that you ask of me?" The Prophet replied, "Go back to your kin until my order reaches you." Abu Dhar said, "In the name of the One Who owns my soul between His hands, I am not going back until I cry out loudly declaring Islam within the mosque!"

After discovering the wonderful new world of Islam, Abu Dhar was being asked to return silently to his kin. Was that even possible for him? He felt it beyond his ability. And so, he entered the Sacred House and cried out as loud as he could, "I bear witness that there is no god but Allah and that Muhammad is His Messenger!"

As far as we know, it was the first public proclamation of Islam and it challenged the arrogance of the Quraysh when it reached their ears. It was cried out by a stranger who did not have any relatives, reputation, or protection in Makkah. He acted out of his own dedication and courage, even though he knew the likely consequences. He was quickly surrounded by the polytheists, who beat him until he fell.

This news reached Al-Abbas, the Prophet's uncle. He came quickly, and could only rescue Abu Dhar using a clever tactic. He told them, "O you Quraysh! You are merchants and your route crosses over Ghifar and this man here is one of their tribesmen. Beware, he may incite his kin against you, provoking them to rob your caravans while passing by." They came back to their senses and left him alone.

Having tasted the sweetness of being hurt in the cause of Allah, Abu Dhar did not want to leave Makkah without being given more. So, on the next day (or some narrations say even on the same day), Abu Dhar encountered two women circling around two idols (Usaf and Nailah) and calling upon them. He stood in front of them and rudely disgraced their idols. The women shouted loudly, and men nearby hastened to beat Abu Dhar until he was unconscious.

When he regained consciousness, he shouted again that there is no god but Allah and Muhammad ﷺ is His Messenger. The Prophet realised the nature of his new disciple and his amazing ability to tackle falsehood head on. However, the time for public declaration of the message had not yet come, so again he ordered Abu Dhar to go back to his kin. Whenever he heard the official announcement of the new religion, he would be sure to play his role.

———◊———

Abu Dhar finally returned to his kin and tribe, telling them about the Prophet ﷺ who called people to worship only Allah and guided them to noble manners. His people embraced Islam one by one. Banu Ghifar alone did not suffice him; he turned also to the people of Aslim to spread the light of Islam there. Time passed by and eventually the Prophet ﷺ and his fellow Muslims settled in Medina.

One day, the city welcomed long lines of people on horseback and on foot. Their feet made such noise that were it not for their loud shout of "Allah is the Greatest", a passer-by would have thought it was an attacking army. The great parade approached and entered Medina. Their destination was the Prophet's mosque. The parade consisted of two tribes, Banu Ghifar and Banu Aslim. Abu Dhar had inspired them all to come to the city of Medina as Muslims: men, women, elderly, youth, even children.

No doubt, the astonishment that the Prophet once felt (when Abu Dhar had first embraced Islam), was multiplied on beholding this sight. The whole tribe had come to Medina after already embracing Islam. And they had already lived several years under the banner of Islam after Allah guided them through Abu Dhar. And now they come together with Banu Aslim. The former notorious highwaymen, had become the allies of truth and great men of good deeds.

Is it not true that Allah guides whom He pleases? The Prophet ﷺ looked at their kind faces, with eyes full of joy, tenderness, and love. He looked at Banu Ghifar and said, "May Allah forgive Ghifar." Then he turned to Banu Aslim and said, "May Allah make peace with Aslim."

Here was Abu Dhar, this magnificent propagator of Islam who was obstinate, unyielding, and difficult to defeat – did the Prophet ﷺ salute him with a special greeting? Indeed, his greeting was blessed and his reward was abundant. Abu Dhar's legacy was going to carry the most honourable of medals - the Prophet's good opinion. The Prophet said of him: "The earth never carried above it, nor did the sky ever shade under it a more truthful tongue than Abu Dhar's".

Muhammad ﷺ determined his Companion's future and summed up his whole life in those simple words. Bold and daring truthfulness was the essence of Abu Dhar's life. Truthfulness of his inner soul, of his faith, and of his tongue. All his life he was truthful, and neither deceived others, nor allowed anyone to deceive him.

His truthfulness was not a mute merit. According to Abu Dhar, truthfulness is never silent. Truthfulness is equivalent to openness and publicity; the publicity of truth and the challenge of falsehood; the support of the right and the refutation of the wrong.

The Prophet ﷺ could see, with his unmistakable insight, all the different difficulties Abu Dhar would have to face because of this disposition towards truth and straightforwardness. He was therefore always ordering him to err on the side of patience. The Prophet once asked him, "O Abu Dhar! What would you do if you witnessed a time when commanders monopolise the war booty?" He replied, "I swear by Allah Who sent you with the truth, I would strike them with my sword!" The Prophet ﷺ said to him, "Shall I guide you to what is better? Be patient till you meet me." Why did the Prophet ask him this specific question? Commanders? Money? It was the cause Abu Dhar was going to devote his life to and the problem he was to encounter with society in the future. The Prophet ﷺ knew it; therefore he asked him this question in order to provide him with this precious advice: "Be patient till you meet me."

Abu Dhar never forgot his teacher and Prophet's instruction. Therefore, he did not carry a sword against those commanders who enriched themselves by taking what was the public money. But also, he did not keep silent, and he did not let them rest. Indeed, although the Prophet ﷺ had forbidden him to carry his sword against them, he had not forbidden him to carry a sharp and truthful tongue. And that is what he did.

———·◊·———

The era of the Prophet ﷺ, and then of Abu Bakr and Umar passed with complete transcendence over all worldly temptations. Even the most greedy souls could not find a way to satisfy their devious desires. In those days there were no deviations that asked for Abu Dhar's usual sharp opposition. As long as Umar, 'Commander of the Faithful' lived, Muslim governors, rulers, and even the wealthy, were forced to live a humble, modest and ascetic life.

No governor of the Caliph (whether in Iraq, Syria, Yemen, or anywhere else in the region) could eat even a sweet if it was unaffordable for ordinary people, without such news reaching Umar. He would immediately order that the governor return to Medina, where he would face his reckoning.

Therefore, Abu Dhar lived happily and with much inward peace during Umar's rule. Nothing ever annoyed Abu Dhar more than the abuse of power and the monopoly of wealth. Umar's firm control over power and his fair distribution of wealth allowed Abu Dhar tranquillity.

It was because of this that he was able to devote himself to Allah's worship and jihad in the cause of Allah. Although he would never keep silent if any infringement was seen here or there, which rarely happened. However, when the great Umar left this world, he left behind a tremendous void and repercussions soon followed.

The Islamic campaigns continued, thus bringing more regions under control. But, at the same time, a longing for ambition and luxury started to float to the surface. In this, Abu Dhar sensed an impending danger. The banners of personal glory were about to tempt those whose role in life was to lift the standard of Allah. Money — created by Allah to allow His servants to benefit mankind - was about to turn into a tyrant master. A master of whom? The Prophet's Companions themselves.

The Prophet ﷺ died with only a pawned shield to his name, although piles of war booty were at his disposal. The excellence of the earth - created by Allah for all human beings and with mutual rights therein - was about to turn into a monopoly and privilege. Power — a responsibility that makes the pious tremble at the thought of the terrible charge in the Hereafter - turned into a means of authority, wealth, and destructive luxury.

Abu Dhar realised all that. And so, he picked up his sword, brandished it and set out to face his society. But soon the echo of the Prophet's ﷺ advice struck his heart, and so he sheathed his weapon. He remembered the Prophet had said that he should not lift his sword in the face of a Muslim: *It is not lawful for a believer to kill another believer except by error* (4:92).

His role was not to fight, but to oppose. The sword was not a means of change; but the truthful, sincere and brave word was. The fair word does not lose its path, and its consequences are not terrifying. The Prophet ﷺ once said, while surrounded by his Companions, that the earth never carried above it, nor did the sky ever shade a more truthful tongue than Abu Dhar's. Why should someone who owns such a truthful tongue and truthful conviction need a sword?

A single word from him hit the target more than any sword. Therefore, Abu Dhar set about meeting certain members of society - the governors, the wealthy, and all those who worshipped the worldly life and relied upon it. It was these individuals who posed a great danger to the religion. This was a religion that came to be a guide, not a tax collector; with prophethood, not dominion; a mercy, not an affliction; to offer humility, not superiority; equality, not differentiation; and satisfaction, not greed. And so it was that Abu Dhar went out to face all those challenges, by himself.

Abu Dhar went out to the strongholds of power and wealth, tackling them one by one. Within a short time, he became the golden standard for the masses. Even in the remote districts where people had not yet met him, word about him got round. He became so well known that he would hardly pass through a land before the powerful and wealthy felt their luxurious lives questioned by his mere presence.

His earnest appeal sounded everywhere he went: "Announce to those who hoard up gold and silver, the warning of branding irons with which their foreheads and bodies will be branded in the Hereafter." He never ascended a mountain, entered a city, or faced a ruler without repeating those same words, so much so that people would welcome him with them, as a chant. This statement turned into a sort of signature for his message to which he devoted his life. He saw wealth being accumulated and monopolised for power, and being turned into a means of supremacy and ultimately abuse. He saw people's overwhelming passion for this life, which threatened to erase the beauty, piety and sincerity built up during the previous years of the Messenger of Allah ﷺ.

When he began his mission, Abu Dhar began with the most authoritative stronghold in Syria, where Muawiyah ibn Abu Sufyan was ruling one of the most fertile lands of Islam. Muawiyah had begun granting and distributing money carelessly, thereby bestowing undeserved privileges upon people of power and rank in order to guarantee his own future. So, it was there that Abu Dhar began, to confront the nucleus of danger before it ruined the entire Islamic way of life.

He donned his humble gown and hastened towards Syria. The people had hardly heard about his arrival before they hurried to welcome him with great enthusiasm, surrounding him wherever he would go. Sharp-eyed, he took a glance at the multitude around him, and noticed that the majority of them were suffering from poverty. He then directed his eyes to a place not too far away where he saw many palaces and landed estates. Then he shouted to those around him, "I wonder why those who don't find something to eat don't go out holding their swords ready to fight?"

But of course, he immediately remembered the Prophet's admonition to replace opposition and rebellion with patience, abandoning the language of war for logic, reason, and conviction. He recalled that the Prophetic way was to teach people that they are all equal like the teeth of a comb; that they are all partners as far as the means of living are concerned; that no one is superior to another except in piety; and that their ruler should be the first to starve if the people suffer hunger, and the last to satisfy his appetite if they become sated.

Abu Dhar decided instead to use his words to sway public opinion. He hoped to stop the rich and wealthy from monopolising class, through intelligence and diplomacy. Within a few days, the whole of Syria resembled a bee-hive that had found its queen. If Abu Dhar had given the slightest gesture for revolt, Syria would have been set alight. But instead he focused on creating a respectable public opinion. His words became the subject of conversation everywhere - inside mosques, during meetings, and even on the roads.

Danger reached its peak for Abu Dhar, when he began speaking about the newly acquired privileges of the rich and powerful. He debated publicly with Muawiyah in front of the masses. Abu Dhar, who possessed the most truthful tongue on earth (as the Prophet ﷺ described), stood up. He asked Muawiyah about his wealth before and after being in power, about the house in which he was living in Makkah, and the castles he owned in Syria. Then he raised the question to the Companions who had accompanied Muawiyah to Syria and who were now also owners of estates and castles.

After that he cried out to them, "Is it you among whom the Prophet lived when the Quran was being revealed?" Then he answered himself, "Yes, it is you! The Quran was revealed among you. It is you who experienced with the Prophet ﷺ all the different scenes." Then he asked them again, "Can't you find this verse in the Book of Allah?...*and those who hoard up gold and silver, and do not expend it in the cause of God, announce to them a painful chastisement. On the Day when it shall be heated in the Fire of Hell, and with their foreheads, and their bodies, and their backs shall be branded. This is what you treasured for yourselves, so taste the evil of what you were treasuring.*" (9:34-35)

Muawiyah tried to argue that this verse was mentioned regarding the People of the Book (i.e. the Jews and Christians). Hereupon Abu Dhar exclaimed, "No, it has been revealed for us all!" Abu Dhar then continued his speech, advising Muawiyah and his followers to give up their landed estates, wealth, and all their possessions, and to abstain from saving for themselves more than their daily need.

Through the people's assemblies, congregations, and meetings, the news of the debate spread and reached everyone's ears. Louder and louder, Abu Dhar's anthem was heard everywhere: "Announce to those who hoard up gold and silver the warning of branding irons." Muawiyah felt the danger of the honourable and rebellious Companion's words, and was terrified. Yet, Muawiyah recognised Abu Dhar's value and did not harm him. Instead, he immediately wrote to the Caliph Uthman, "Abu Dhar spoils the people in Syria."

Uthman sent for Abu Dhar, asking him to come to Medina. On his departure, Abu Dhar set off from Syria and the people there sent him away with kindness, affection, and honour. His farewell party was like no other Damascus has seen since.

---·◦·---

"I don't need your world!" That is what Abu Dhar said to the Caliph Uthman after he reached Medina and a prolonged conversation took place between them. News was coming from all regions that Abu Dhar's opinions had actually agitated the masses throughout the Muslim world. It was at that time that Uthman began to truly realise the actual danger of Abu Dhar's opinion and its strength. He therefore decided to keep him beside him at Medina.

Uthman presented his decision to him in a friendly way: "Stay here beside me. You will be endowed with blessings day and night." But of course, Abu Dhar said, "I don't need your world!" Indeed, he did not need the people's world. He was one of those rare individuals who searched for the enrichment of their soul, dedicating his life to giving, not receiving. He asked the Caliph Uthman to allow him to go out to Ar-Rabadhah, and he allowed him.

Despite his fierce opposition on certain matters, Abu Dhar stayed close to the way of Allah and His Prophet ﷺ, always keeping close to the Prophet's advice to never carry a sword. It was as if the Messenger had seen Abu Dhar's future, and so he bestowed upon him this precious advice.

He may have disagreed with the leadership in some regards, but Abu Dhar never liked those who sought to ignite the flames of civil strife for their own ends. One day, while in Ar-Rabadhah, a delegation from Kufa came to ask him to help them revolt against the Caliph. He drove them back with his decisive words: "By Allah, if Uthman was to crucify me on the longest board or on a mountain, I would patiently obey, for Allah's reward would be waiting for me, and I see it to be the best for me. And if he was to force me to walk from one end of the horizon to the other, I would patiently obey, for Allah's reward would be waiting for me, and I see it to be the best for me. And if he was to force me back to my home I would patiently obey, for Allah's reward would be waiting for me, and I see it to be the best for me."

He was a man who was not interested in any worldly gain, he was truly blessed with a unique insight from Allah. He realised again the tremendous danger involved in armed civil strife; therefore, he abstained from it. But he also realised the tremendous danger involved in silence; therefore, he abstained from that too. That is why he continued to raise his voice, not his sword.

He was not tempted by greedy desires, nor hindered by worldly obstacles. Abu Dhar kept himself busy with and devoted himself to sincere, honest opposition. He spent his whole life focusing on the faults of power and money. Abu Dhar was afraid his brethren would fall into their traps - the same brethren who had carried the standard of Islam with the Prophet ﷺ not so long ago, and whom he wanted to remain the carriers of the Prophet's message ﷺ.

Power and money were, furthermore, the backbone of societies and communities. If misused, the people's destiny would be in danger. Abu Dhar wished so much that the Prophet's Companions would not be appointed as governors and would not collect fortunes, but would rather stay as they always had been: as spiritual guides to the right path for Allah's worshippers. He knew well the voracity of life and the voracity of money, and he knew that both his and Umar's examples would never be repeated! How often did he hear the Prophet ﷺ asking his Companions to be aware of the temptation of authority saying, "It's a deposition in trust, and on the Day of Resurrection it will be a shame and regret except to the one who was endowed with it justly, and accomplished his duty."

Abu Dhar went so far that he avoided his brethren (if he did not boycott them), for no other reason than that they had become rulers and, of course, had therefore become wealthier. Abu Musa Al-Ash'ari once met him. He had hardly seen him when he stretched out his arms with joy and delight shouting, "Welcome Abu Dhar! Welcome my brother!" But Abu Dhar held himself back saying, "I am not your brother; I was so before you became an administrator and governor."

In the same way, Abu Hurairah once met and embraced him in welcome, but Abu Dhar pushed him back and said, "Isn't it you who became governor, then extended your buildings and possessed plantations and cattle?" Abu Hurairah defended himself, trying to prove his innocence and refute those rumours.

It may seem that Abu Dhar held an extreme position towards power and wealth, but his logic was shaped by his sincerity to himself and to his faith. Thus, Abu Dhar stood by his deeds, behaviour, and views according to the same standard that the Prophet ﷺ and his two Companions, Abu Bakr and Umar, had left behind. If some people saw that standard to be an out-of-reach ideal, Abu Dhar saw it to be a normative example. An example charting a path for life, particularly for those who had actually interacted with the Prophet ﷺ, prayed behind him, taken part in jihad with him, and sworn the oath of allegiance to him.

Also, of course, his inspired intellect knew the decisive influence of power and property in determining people's destiny. Therefore, anything that could taint the trustworthiness of power or the fairness of wealth, represented an imminent danger that demanded opposition.

As long as he lived, Abu Dhar upheld the standard of the Prophet ﷺ and his two Companions' good example. He was a great figure in the art of predominance over the temptation of power and wealth. The governorship of Iraq was once offered to him, but he said, "By Allah, you will never tempt me with your world."

Once, one of his companions saw him wearing an old gown and asked him, "Don't you have another one? I saw you a couple of days ago with two other gowns in your hands." Abu Dhar replied, "O cousin! I gave them to someone who needed them more than I do." He said to him, "By Allah, you need them!" Abu Dhar then answered, "May Allah forgive us. You glorify this life! Can't you see that I am wearing a gown? And I own another one for the congregational Friday prayer. Moreover, I own a goat which I milk and a donkey which I ride. Is there a better blessing?"

He once sat down talking to people and said, "My friend advised me to do seven things:

1. He asked me to love the poor and to get closer to them.
2. He asked me to look to those who are inferior and not to those who are superior.
3. He asked me never to ask anyone for anything (i.e. to abstain from begging).
4. He asked me to be kind to my relatives.
5. He asked me to say the truth, no matter how sour it may be.
6. He asked me never to be afraid of a critic's censure.
7. And he asked me to frequently say, 'There is no power nor might except Allah's."

Abu Dhar lived according to this Prophetic advice until he became a living conscience moving amongst his own people. Imam Ali once said, "There is no one nowadays who is nonchalant about people's criticism - as far as Allah and His rules are concerned - except Abu Dhar." He lived in complete opposition of the abuse of power and the monopoly of property. He lived resisting all that was wrong and building all that was right. He lived devoted to the responsibility of good advice and warning. When he was hindered from spelling out his fatwa (formal legal opinion in Islamic law), he raised his voice and said to those hindering him, "By the name of the One in Whose hands my soul is, if you put the sword to my neck and I still thought that I could carry out a word I've heard from the Prophet ﷺ before you, I would carry it out."

Had the Muslims listened to his advice on that day, a lot of civil strife and turmoil would have been prevented. The whole Muslim nation soon faced rebellion and alarming danger. But by this point Abu Dhar was suffering the agonies of death in Ar-Rabadhah, the place where he chose to stay after his disagreement with Uthman. Let us bid him farewell and see how the last scene of his admirable life played out.

The slim, dark-skinned woman sitting crying beside Abu Dhar is his wife. He is asking her, "Why do you cry [when] death is true?" She answers in tears: "You are dying and I don't have a gown which suffices to be a shroud!" He smiles warmly and says to her "Calm down. Don't cry. I heard the Prophet ﷺ once saying while I was sitting among a number of Companions, 'One of you will die in a desert land, and a group of the faithful will witness him.' All those who were sitting with me at that assembly have died, whether in a village or among a congregation. No one is left except me, and now I am dying in a desert land. Watch and see, a group of the faithful will soon show up. By Allah, I have never lied in my life." And with that, he soon passed, blessed as he was.

Elsewhere, there is a caravan on a journey across the desert. It consists of a group of the faithful, with Abdullah ibn Masud (the Prophet's Companion) at their head. Ibn Masud could see the scene before he reached it: that of an outstretched body - like a dead person - and a crying woman and boy beside it. He redirects his camel's bridle and the whole caravan follows him towards the scene. He has hardly taken a look at the dead body, when he realises that it is his companion and brother in Islam, Abu Dhar.

His tears roll down freely while he stands in front of this virtuous man saying, "The Messenger of Allah was truthful. You will walk alone, die alone, and resurrect alone." Ibn Masud narrated the interpretation of the statement "You will walk alone, die alone, and resurrect alone," to his companions:

"It was in the ninth year after hijra, during the Battle of Tabuk, when the Prophet ﷺ had ordered us to fully prepare to meet the Romans (who had begun to carry out their conspiracies and cunning tricks against Islam). Those days when people were asked to go out for jihad were very distressing and hard. The destination was far away, and the enemy terrifying.

A group of Muslims refrained from going forth, justifying their position with different apologies. The Prophet ﷺ and his Companions went forth. The farther they went, the more exhausted and tired they became. Whenever a man stayed behind people said, 'O Prophet! So-and-so stayed behind.' He said, 'Let him! If he's any good, he will reach you. If he's something else, then Allah will save you his trouble.'

One day the people turned around. They could not find Abu Dhar. They told the Prophet ﷺ that Abu Dhar had stayed behind and his camel had slowed down. It is here that the Prophet ﷺ repeated his first statement. Abu Dhar's camel had become weaker under the severe pressure of hunger, thirst, and hot weather. It stumbled due to weakness and fatigue. Abu Dhar tried by all means to force it to move forward, but the burden of the camel's exhaustion was too heavy.

Finally, Abu Dhar felt that he would be left behind, losing the caravan's traces. Therefore, he dismounted from his camel, took his belongings, carried them on his back, and continued his route on foot over the burning desert sand, hurrying in order to rejoin the Prophet ﷺ and his Companions.

In the early morning, when the Muslims had stopped for a while to rest, one of them saw a cloud of dust and sand, behind which the shadow of a man could be seen. The one who saw that said to the Prophet ﷺ, 'O Messenger of Allah, there is someone walking alone.' The Prophet said, 'It is Abu Dhar'.

The Muslims continued their talk until the man crossed the remaining distance between them. Only then were they able to know who he was. The respectful traveller approached little by little. Although he could only with great effort pull his feet out of the burning sand and, with a lot of pain, carry the heavy burden on his back. He was delighted to have finally reached the blessed caravan without staying behind and abandoning the Prophet ﷺ and his Companions.

When he at last reached the caravan, someone shouted, 'O Prophet, it's Abu Dhar.' Abu Dhar headed towards the Prophet ﷺ. The Prophet had hardly seen him, when he tenderly, kindly, and sadly smiled and said, 'Allah will have mercy upon Abu Dhar. He walks alone, dies alone, and resurrects alone'."

―――――•◊•―――――

Twenty years or more had passed since that event, but Ibn Masud still remembered how the Prophet had described Abu Dhar. He died alone in the desert of Ar-Rabadhah, having walked on his own individual, glorious path. He is remembered by history for his brave resistance and his great asceticism. And Allah will indeed resurrect him alone, because his numerous merits mean that no one else could ever find a place near him.

(4)

BILAL IBN RABAH

Confronting and Overcoming Horrors

Whenever Umar ibn Al Khattab mentioned Abu Bakr he would say, "Abu Bakr is our master and the emancipator of our master." That is to say, the emancipator of Bilal. Indeed, the man given the agnomen 'our master' by Umar must be a great man. However, this man - who was dark in complexion, slender, very tall, thick-haired and with a sparse beard (as described by narrators) - would hardly hear such words of praise without bending his head in humility. Bilal would lower his gaze and say through tears, "Indeed, I am an Abyssinian. Yesterday, I was only a slave!"

So, who is this Abyssinian who was only yesterday 'a slave'? He is none other than Bilal ibn Rabah, the caller to prayer and troublemaker to the idols. He was one of Islam's great miracles of faith. There are hundreds of millions of people throughout the centuries and generations who know Bilal's name and his role, just as they know the Caliphs.

Even if you ask a Muslim child "Who is Bilal?" - whether you're in the depths of Africa, the mountains of Asia, the vast Americas, or indeed anywhere where Muslims reside - he will know who he was. He will answer you, "He was the muezzin of the Messenger ﷺ". He was also the former slave, whose master used to torture him with burning hot stones to force him to apostatise. But he refused and only said, "One…One".

Whenever you consider the enduring fame that Islam bestowed upon Bilal, you should know that before Islam this man was simply a slave who tended herds of camels for his master, in exchange for a mere handful of dates. Had it not been for Islam, it would have been his fate to remain enslaved, wandering among the crowd until death brought an end to his life and caused him to perish forgotten.

However, his faith proved to be true, and the magnificence of the religion which he believed in gave him an elevated status during his lifetime. He earned a respected place among the great and holy men of Islamic history. Indeed, many human beings of distinction, prestige, or wealth have not obtained even one-tenth of Bilal's immortal reputation.

Indeed, his modest lineage and his position as a slave did not deprive him of status when he chose to embrace Islam. Instead, he occupied the highest place of truthfulness, purity, and self-sacrifice.

People thought that a slave like Bilal — who had neither kinfolk nor power, who did not possess any control over his life (but was himself a possession of his master), who came and went amid the sheep, camels, and other livestock of his master – would become anything. But he went beyond all expectations and possessed faith like no other. He was the first muezzin, both of the Messenger and of Islam, a much coveted position by all the nobles of Quraysh who had also embraced Islam. Yes, this was Bilal ibn Rabah.

Ethnically, Bilal was a black Abyssinian. His fate led him into a life of slavery, and he found himself in the ownership of the tribe of Jumah in Makkah, where his mother was also one of their slave girls. He led the life of a slave, whose bleak days were all alike, with no right over his day and no hope for his tomorrow.

The news of Muhammad's call reached his ears when the Makkans began to talk about him. He would listen to the discussions of his master and his guests, especially Umayah ibn Khalaf, one of the elders of the Banu Jumah. Very often, Umayah and his master's companions spoke about the Messenger ﷺ with words filled with anxiety, rage, and malice. Amid the furious words, Bilal on the other hand was slowly picking up on the attributes of this new religion. He began to admire the qualities of Islam and during the threatening speech he overheard, he also caught their acknowledgement of Muhammad's nobility, truthfulness, and loyalty. Sometimes, he even heard them amazed at what Muhammad had come with. They said to one another, "Muhammad was never a liar, magician, or mad, but we have to describe him this way until we turn away from him those who rush to his religion."

He heard them talking about his honesty, his nobility, his purity and his composure of intelligence. Furthermore, Bilal heard them whispering about the reasons that made them challenge and antagonise him: first, their allegiance to the religion of their fathers; second, their fear over the glory of the Quraysh (initially bestowed upon them because of their religious status as a centre of idol worship for the whole of the Arabian Peninsula); third, their envy of Muhammad's tribe, Banu Hashim, namely that anyone from them should claim to be a prophet or messenger.

One day, Bilal ibn Rabah recognised the light of Allah and heard His resonance in the depths of his good soul. So, he went to the Messenger of Allah ﷺ and converted to Islam. It did not take long before the news of his embracing Islam spread. It was a shock to the chiefs of the Banu Jumah, who were very proud. The devils of the earth sat couched over Umayah ibn Khalaf, who considered the acceptance of Islam by one of their slaves an overwhelming blow filled with shame and disgrace. Their Abyssinian slave had converted to Islam and followed Muhammad ﷺ? Umayah said to himself, "It does not matter. Indeed, the sun this day shall not set but with the Islam of this stray slave." The sun never did set with the Islam of Bilal, but it set one day with all the idols of the Quraysh and the patrons of paganism among them.

———•◊•———

As for Bilal, he adopted an attitude that would honour not only Islam (even though Islam was more worthy of it), but also all of humanity. He resisted the harshest kind of torture. Allah made him proof of the fact that the colour of one's skin and the ties of bondage do not reduce the greatness of a soul if it has found faith, adhered to its Creator, and clung to its right.

Bilal gave a profound lesson to those both in his age and every age thereafter; to those of his religion and every other religion. It was the idea that freedom and supremacy of conscience could not be bartered, neither for gold nor punishment. He was stripped naked and laid on hot coals to make him renounce his religion, but still he refused.

The Messenger ﷺ and Islam made this weak Abyssinian slave into a teacher. He taught all humanity the art of respecting one's conscience, and how to defend its freedom. They used to take him out in the midday heat when the desert had turned hellish. Then they would throw him naked on its scorching rocks, bring a burning hot rock (which took several men to lift) and throw it onto his body and chest. This savage torture was repeated every day until some of his executioners took pity on him. Finally, they agreed to set him free on the condition that he would speak well of their gods, even with only one word. This would have allowed them to preserve their pride, and prevent the Quraysh from saying that their tribe had been humiliated by the resistance of a determined slave.

But even this one word, which he could have easily said without conviction, Bilal still refused to say. Instead, he began repeating his chant of, "One...One!" His torturers shouted at him, imploring him, "Say the name of Al-Lat and Al-Uzza." But he only answered, "One...One" They said to him, "Say as we say." But he answered them with caustic irony, "Indeed my tongue is not good at that."

And so, Bilal remained in the melting heat, under the weight of the heavy rock, and by sunset they raised him up and put a rope around his neck. Then they ordered their boys to take him around the mountains and streets of Makkah. All the while Bilal's tongue said only, "One...One."

When the night overtook them, they began bargaining with him, "Tomorrow, speak well of our gods, say, 'My lord is Al-Lat and Al-Uzza, and we'll leave you alone. We are tired of torturing you, as if we are the tortured ones." But he shook his head and said, "One...One." So, Umayah ibn Khalaf kicked him and exploded with exasperation: "What bad luck has thrown you upon us, O slave of evil? By Al-Lat and Al-Uzza, I'll make you an example for slaves and masters."

After being calmed down again, Umayah decided to continue Bilal's torture the next day. As midday approached, Bilal was taken to the sun-baked ground. He was patient, brave, firm, and expecting the reward in the Hereafter. Abu Bakr Al-Siddiq went to them while they were torturing him and shouted at them, "Are you killing a man because he says, 'Allah is my Lord?'" Then he shouted at Umayah ibn Khalaf, "Take more than his price and set him free." It was as if Umayah were drowning and had caught a lifeboat. It was to his liking and he was very much pleased when he heard Abu Bakr offering the price of his freedom, since they had despaired of subjugating Bilal. And as they were merchants, they realised that selling him was more profitable to them than killing him.

Therefore, they sold him to Abu Bakr, and he emancipated him immediately, so Bilal finally took his place among free men. When Al-Siddiq put his arm round Bilal, rushing with him to freedom, Umayah said to him, "Take him, for by Al-Lat and Al-Uzza if you had refused to buy him except for one ounce of gold, I would have sold him to you." Abu Bakr realised the bitterness of despair and disappointment hidden in these words. It was appropriate not to answer, but because they violated the dignity of this man who had become his brother and his equal, he answered Umayah saying, "By Allah, if you had refused to sell him except for a hundred ounces, I would have paid it." He departed with his companion to the Messenger of Allah, giving him news of his liberation, and there was a great celebration.

After the Muslims made hijra to Medina and settled there, the Messenger ﷺ instituted the adhan. So, who would become the muezzin five times a day? Who would call across the land, "Allah is the Greatest" and "There is no god but Allah"?

It was Bilal, who had shouted out 13 years before during his torture, "Allah is One...One." He was chosen by the Messenger that day to be the first muezzin in Islam. With his melodious soul-stirring voice, he filled the hearts with faith and ears with awe when he called:

Allah is the Greatest, Allah is the Greatest
Allah is the Greatest, Allah is the Greatest
I bear witness that there is no god but Allah
I bear witness that there is no god but Allah
I bear witness that Muhammad is the Messenger of Allah
I bear witness that Muhammad is the Messenger of Allah
Come to Prayer, Come to Prayer
Come to Success, Come to Success
Allah is the Greatest, Allah is the Greatest
There is no god but Allah

Fighting soon broke out when the army of the Quraysh came to invade Medina. The war raged fiercely and Bilal was amongst those attacking in this first battle. Islam had been plunged into the Battle of Badr, whose motto the Messenger ﷺ ordered to be, "One...One."

In this battle, the Quraysh sacrificed their youth and all their noblemen to their own hunger for destruction. Umayah ibn Khalaf (who had been Bilal's master and who had tortured him brutally) was reluctant to fight. But his friend Uqbah ibn Abi Mu'ayt went to him when he heard the news of his withdrawal, carrying an incense censer in his right hand. When he arrived Umayah was sitting among his people. Uqbah threw the censer between his hands and said to him, "O Abu Ali, use this. You are one of the women." But Umayah shouted at him saying, "May Allah make you and what you came with ugly!" He had not found a way out of the matter, and so he was compelled to go out and fight.

Uqbah had been the greatest supporter of Umayah in the torture of Bilal and other weak Muslims. On that day, he himself was the one who urged Umayah to go to the Battle of Badr where they would both perish. Umayah had been shirking away from the war. Had it not been for what Uqbah did to shame him, he would not have gone out to battle, and to his death.

But Allah executes His command. So, Umayah went out, because there was an outstanding issue between him and one Allah's servants. It was time to settle it. Indeed destiny mocked these tyrants, because by whose hand did Umayah fall? By the hand of Bilal himself and Bilal alone! The same hands that Umayah used to chain, who he beat and tortured, those very hands had an appointment with destiny.

When the fighting began between the two sides, and the side of the Muslims shouted the motto, "One...One," the heart of Umayah was perturbed, and a warning came to him. The word which his slave used to repeat yesterday under abject torture, had become today the motto of an entire religion and nation: "One...One".

———•◇•———

The swords clashed in the battle and the fighting became more intense. As the battle neared its end, Umayah ibn Khalaf noticed Abdur Rahman ibn Awf, a Companion of the Messenger of Allah ﷺ. He sought refuge with him and asked to be his captive, in the hope of saving his own life. Abdur Rahman was his old friend before Islam and he accepted his plea and granted him refuge. Then he took Umayah and walked with him amidst the battle to the place where captives were held.

On the way Bilal noticed him and shouted, "The head of kufr (disbelief), Umayah ibn Khalaf! May I not be saved if he is saved!" He lifted up his sword to cut off his arrogant head, but Abdur Rahman shouted to him, "O Bilal, he is my captive!" A captive while the war was still raging? A captive while his sword was still dripping with the blood of dead Muslims? Surely not. In Bilal's opinion, this was an abuse of the system, and Umayah had scoffed and abused them enough.

Bilal realised that he alone would not be able to storm the sanctuary of his brother, Abdur Rahman. So, he shouted at the top of his voice to the Muslims, "O helpers of Allah! The head of kufr, Umayah ibn Khalaf!

May I not be saved if he is saved!" A band of Muslims approached with swords in their hand. They surrounded Umayah, and his son who was also fighting with the Quraysh. Abdur Rahman ibn Awf was powerless to stop them. Bilal watched on as the body of Umayah fell beneath their swords. Then he hastened away from him shouting, "One...One."

I do not think it is our right to examine the virtue of leniency on this occasion. If the meeting between Bilal and Umayah had taken place in other circumstances, Bilal may well have been asked to exercise leniency, and a man with his piety would not have withheld it. But the meeting which took place between them was in the middle of a war, where each party came to destroy its enemy, swords ablaze. Then Bilal saw Umayah, the man who had left no spot on Bilal's body free from his torture. Where and how did he see him? He saw him in the arena of battle, mowing down all the Muslim heads that he could. If he had reached Bilal's, he too would have met his death. In such circumstances, it was arguably fair that Bilal chose not to exercise forgiveness. But, Allah knows best.

And so, the days went by and Makkah was eventually conquered. The Messenger ﷺ led 10,000 Muslims into the city peacefully, saying in thanks, "Allah is the Greatest". He headed for the Kaba immediately, the holy place which the Quraysh had crowded with as many idols as there were days in the year. "The truth has come and falsehood has vanished," he pronounced.

Ever since that day, there has been no Uzza, no Lat and no Hubal. In good conscience, people could worship no one but Allah, Who has no likeness, the One, the Most Great, the Most High. The Messenger entered the Kaba accompanied by Bilal. He had hardly entered it when he faced a carved idol representing Ibrahim ﷺ prophesising with sticks.

The Messenger ﷺ was angry and said, "May Allah [strike them down]. Our ancestor never prophesised with sticks. Ibrahim was not a Jew or Christian, but he was a true Muslim and was never a polytheist." Then he ordered Bilal to ascend to the top of the mosque to perform the call to prayer, and so Bilal called the adhan. How magnificent was the time, place, and occasion!

Life came to a standstill in Makkah, and thousands of Muslims stood like motionless air, repeating in submissiveness and whispering the words of the adhan after Bilal. Meanwhile, the polytheists were in their homes hardly believing what was happening. They must have thought, "Was this Muhammad ﷺ and his poor followers who were expelled only recently from their homes? Was this really him, with 10,000 of his believers? Was this really him, whom we chased away, fighting and killing his most beloved kin? Was this really him, who was speaking to us a few minutes ago while our necks were at his mercy, saying, 'Go, you are free'?"

Three nobles of the Quraysh were sitting in the open space in front of the Kaba. These three were Abu Sufyan ibn Harb, who had embraced Islam only hours ago, Attab ibn Usaid and Al-Harith ibn Hisham, who had not yet embraced Islam. Attab, with his eyes on Bilal crying out the adhan, said, "Allah has honoured Usaid in that he did not hear this, or else he would have heard what would infuriate him." Al-Harith said, "By Allah, if I were sure that Muhammad ﷺ is telling the truth, I would follow him." Abu Sufyan cleverly said, "I am not saying a word, for if I do, these pebbles will inform about me."

When the Prophet left the Kaba he saw them and read their faces instantly. He said, with his eyes shining from the light of Allah and the joy of victory, "I know what you've said," and he told them what they had said. Al-Harith and Attab shouted, "We bear witness that you are the Messenger of Allah. By Allah, no one heard us, so we can't say somebody informed you!"

———.◊.———

Bilal lived with the Messenger of Allah ﷺ, witnessing all their battles, calling to prayer and observing the rites of this great religion that took him out of darkness to light, from servitude to freedom. The stature of Islam along with the stature of Muslims was elevated. Every day Bilal was getting closer to the Messenger of Allah, who used to describe him as "one of the inhabitants of Paradise."

But Bilal remained just as he was, noble and humble, always considering himself "the Abyssinian who only yesterday was a slave." One day he was proposing to two girls for himself and for his brother, so he said to their father, "I am Bilal and this is my brother, two slaves from

Abyssinia. We were astray and Allah guided us. We were two slaves and Allah emancipated us. If you agree on us marrying your daughters, all praise is to Allah; if you refuse, then Allah is the Greatest."

After the Messenger ﷺ passed away, Abu Bakr Al-Siddiq took the command of the Muslims. Bilal went to the Prophet's successor and said to him, "O Caliph of the Messenger of Allah, I heard the Messenger of Allah ﷺ say, 'The best deed of a believer is jihad in the cause of Allah'." Abu Bakr said, "So what do you want, Bilal?" He replied, "I want to defend the cause of Allah until I die." Abu Bakr said, "And who will call the adhan for us?" Bilal said, with his eyes overflowing with tears, "I will not call the adhan for anyone after the Messenger of Allah." Abu Bakr said, "Stay and call to prayer for us, Bilal." He replied, "If you liberated me to be for you, I will do what you want, but if you liberated me for Allah, leave me to whom I was emancipated for." Abu Bakr said, "I emancipated you for Allah, Bilal."

The narrators differ on what happened next. Some of them believe that Bilal travelled and continued to defend Islam in battle. Others narrate that he accepted Abu Bakr's request to stay with him in Medina. When Abu Bakr died and Umar succeeded him, Bilal asked his permission to go to Syria. Bilal dedicated the remaining years of his life to fighting in the cause of Islam, determined to meet Allah and His Messenger after doing the deed most beloved to them. His melodious, welcoming and awe-inspiring voice no longer called the adhan, because whenever he uttered in his call, "I bear witness that Muhammad ﷺ is the Messenger of Allah," memories would stir in him, and his voice would vanish under his sadness.

His last adhan was during the days of Umar, the Commander of the Faithful, when he visited Syria. The Muslims entreated him to persuade Bilal to call one adhan for them. The Commander of the Faithful called Bilal when it was time for prayer and pleaded with him to make the adhan - Bilal acquiesced. The Companions of the Messenger of Allah ﷺ who were with the Commander of the Faithful while Bilal was calling the adhan, wept as they never did before - Caliph Umar the most.

Bilal eventually died in Syria, fighting in the cause of Allah just as he had wanted. Beneath the dust of Damascus, there lays the body of one of the greatest men of mankind. A man who stood up for the creed of Islam with true conviction.

(5)

ABDULLAH IBN UMAR

The Repentant Servant of Allah

At the peak of his long life, Abdullah said, "I swore the oath of allegiance to the Prophet ﷺ. I have never broken my oath, nor have I turned to something else to this day. I never swore allegiance to those in civil strife, nor did I awake a sleeping Muslim."

These words are an accurate summary of the life of the virtuous man, Abdullah ibn Umar. Although he lived past the age of 80, his relationship with Islam and the Prophet first began when he was only 13 years old. He had accompanied his father to the battle of Badr, hoping to have a place among the Mujahidun, but was sent back by the Prophet due to his young age. Since that day - and even before that when he accompanied his father on his hijra to Medina - that mature young boy began his journey with the Prophet of Islam ﷺ.

From that day, until the day he passed (at the age of 85) Abdullah was always a persistent and repentant man; never deviating from his path, not even by a hair's breadth. He never broke the oath of allegiance which he had sworn, nor did he break any other pledge he made. The merits of Abdullah ibn Umar, are abundant and dazzling. Among these are his knowledge, modesty, the straightness of his conscience, his generosity, piety, persistence in worship, and his sincere adherence to the Prophet's example. By means of all these merits and qualities, Ibn Umar shaped his unique personality, and his sincere and truthful life.

He learned a lot of good manners from his father, Umar ibn Al-Khattab, and together both father and son learned their manners and noble virtues from the Prophet ﷺ himself. Like his father, his belief in Allah and His Prophet was perfect; therefore, the way in which he pursued the Prophet's steps was nothing but admirable. He was always looking at what the Prophet was doing in every matter, and then humbly imitated his deeds to the finest detail. For example, wherever the Prophet prayed, Ibn Umar also prayed, on the very same spot. If the Prophet ﷺ invoked Allah while standing, then Ibn Umar would invoke Allah standing up. If the Prophet invoked Allah while sitting, so too would Ibn Umar. On the same particular route where the Prophet once dismounted from his camel and prayed two rakahs, Ibn Umar would do the same while traveling to the same place.

Moreover, he remembered that the Prophet's camel turned twice at a certain spot in Makkah before the Prophet dismounted and before his two rakahs of prayer. The camel may have done that spontaneously to prepare itself a suitable halting place, but Ibn Umar would reach that spot, turn his camel in a circle, then allow it to kneel down. After that he would pray two rakahs in exactly the same manner he had seen the Prophet. Such exaggerated imitation even made Aisha remark once: "No one followed the Prophet's steps in his coming and going as Ibn Umar did."

He spent his long, blessed life and his firm loyalty adhering to the Prophet's Sunnah. So much so that the virtuous Muslims beseeched Allah: "O Allah, save Ibn Umar as long as I live so that I can follow him. I don't know anyone still adhering to the early traditions except him."

Similar to that strong and firm adherence to each of the Prophet's steps and practice (Sunnah) was Ibn Umar's respect for the Prophetic traditions (hadith). He never related a hadith unless he remembered it to the letter. His contemporaries said, "None of the Companions of the Prophet was more cautious not to add or subtract something from a hadith than Abdullah ibn Umar." In the same way he was very cautious when giving a fatwa. One day somebody came to ask him for a fatwa. When he put forward his question, Ibn Umar answered, "I have no knowledge concerning what you are asking about." The man was on his way out. Hardly had he left the place when Ibn Umar rubbed his hands happily and said to himself, "Ibn Umar has been asked about what he does not know, and so he replied, 'I don't know!'"

He was very much afraid to perform ijtihad (independent judgment on a legal question) in his fatwas. He was living according to the instructions of a great religion - a religion which grants a reward to the one who makes a mistake, and two rewards to the one who comes up with a correct fatwa. However, Ibn Umar's piety deprived him of the courage to make any such fatwa.

In the same way, Abdullah Ibn Umar also refrained from taking the post of a judge. The position of a judge was one of the highest roles in society, guaranteeing wealth, prestige, and glory. But why should the pious Ibn Umar need such things? The Caliph Uthman once sent for him personally and asked him to hold the position of judge, but he politely declined. Uthman asked him, "Do you disobey me?" Ibn Umar answered, "No, but it came to my knowledge that judges are of three kinds. One who judges ignorantly: he is in hell; one who judges according to his desire: he is in hell; one who involves himself in making ijtihad and is unerring in his judgment. That one will turn empty-handed, no sin committed and no reward to be granted. I ask you by Allah to exempt me." Uthman exempted him, but only after he pledged never to tell anyone about this. Uthman knew Ibn Umar's place in people's hearts, and he was afraid that if the pious knew why he had declined, they too would follow suit, and then the Caliph would never find a virtuous judge.

It may seem as if Ibn Umar's stance was a passive one. However, it was not so. His restraint and abstention did not paralyse the function of jurisdiction, nor did it mean his alternate would be unqualified. Therefore, safe in that knowledge, Ibn Umar preferred to devote his time to purifying his soul through worship and obedience. Furthermore, in that period of Islamic history, life became more comfortable and luxurious, money more abundant, positions and authoritative ranks more available. The temptation of money and authority began to enter the hearts of the faithful, which made some of the Prophet's Companions - Ibn Umar among them – even more determined to resist that temptation. How? By making themselves models of worship and piety.

Ibn Umar made himself a 'friend of the night', by praying at night, crying, and asking forgiveness during its latter hours before daybreak. He had once, during his youth, seen a dream. The Prophet ﷺ interpreted it in a way which made the night prayer a source of hope and delight for Abdullah. Let us listen to him as he narrates the story of his dream: "During the Prophetic era, I saw a dream in which I was riding a piece of brocade which let me fly to any place in Paradise I wished. Then I saw two [individuals] approaching me, intending to take me to hell, but an angel met them saying, 'Don't be afraid', so they left me. My sister Hafsa narrated the dream to the Prophet ﷺ, who said, 'What an excellent man Abdullah is. If he is praying at night, then let him pray more'."

From that day until he returned to Allah, he never stopped performing his night prayer, neither while home, nor while traveling. He was frequently praying, reciting the Quran, and praising Allah. Like his father, his tears rolled down abundantly whenever he heard a warning from a verse in the Quran.

Ubaid ibn Umar said: "I was once reading to Abdullah Ibn Umar this verse: *How will it be for them when We bring from every nation a witness, and bring you to witness over them all? On that day those who disbelieved and disobeyed the Messenger will wish the earth to be split open and swallow them, but they will never conceal from Allah any of their saying* (4:41-42). Ibn Umar began to cry till his beard was wet from tears."

Another day, he was sitting among his brothers reading the Quranic verse: *Woe to those who give insufficient measure, who when others measure for them they make full measure, but when they measure out, or weigh out for others, they give less than due, Do such not think that they shall be raised up on a Mighty Day? The Day when all mankind shall stand before the Lord of the Worlds* (83:1-6). Then Ibn Umar repeated again and again, *The Day when all mankind shall stand before the Lord of the Worlds*, and tears rolled down his face as if they were heavy rain from the sky.

His generosity, asceticism and piety all worked together in complete harmony to shape the most magnificent merits of a great man. He gave abundantly to others, often donating very fine (halal) things because, as an ascetic, he never cared if his generosity left him poor. Ibn Umar was one of those who had high incomes. He was a successful, honest merchant for a greater part of his life, and his income from the treasury (Bait Al-Mal) was abundant. However, he never saved that money for himself, but always spent it copiously on the poor and needy.

Ayub ibn Wail Ar-Rassiby tells us about one of his generous acts in a story he narrated. One day, Ibn Umar was granted 4,000 dirhams and a piece of velvet. The next day Ayub saw him in the market buying his camel some fodder on credit. Ayub went to his house asking his close relatives, "Wasn't Abu Abdur Rahman (i.e. Abdullah ibn Umar) granted 4,000 dirhams and a piece of velvet yesterday?" They said, "Yes." He then told them that he had seen him in the market buying fodder for his camel and could not find money for it. They told him, "He didn't go to sleep before distributing all of it, then he carried the velvet on his back and went out. When he returned, it wasn't with him. We asked him about it, and he said, 'I gave it to a poor person.'" Ibn Wail went out shaking his head until he entered the market. There he climbed to a higher ground and shouted to the people, "O merchants, what do you do with your life? Here is Ibn Umar who has been granted 4,000 dirhams, so he distributes them, then the next morning he buys fodder for his camel on credit?!"

Of course, with Muhammad ﷺ himself as a tutor and Umar as his father, Ibn Umar had all the foundations of a great man. His respect, good behaviour, and admiration towards his father was obvious. Umar's personality forced his foes, his relatives, and, above all, his sons to pay him respect. One who belonged to the Prophet ﷺ and to that kind of father would arguably never have been a slave to money. That is why this story from Ayub is on par with his character.

His generosity was never a means of arrogance. He always dedicated himself to the needy, rarely eating his meal alone - orphans and poor people were always present. He often reprimanded some of his sons when they invited the rich, and not the poor ones, to their banquets, thereupon saying, "You leave the hungry behind and invite the sated ones." The poor knew his tenderness, felt his kindness and sympathy, so they often crossed his path for him to take them to his home. When they saw him, he was like a sweet-scented flower surrounded by a drove of bees seeking its nectar.

Money in his hands was his slave, not his master; a means for necessity, and not luxury. His money was not his alone. The poor had a right to it, a mutually corresponding right, with no privilege kept for himself. His self-denial helped him to reach such great levels of generosity that he never had any real interest in the worldly life. On the contrary, he wished nothing more than to possess a gown for his clothing, and just enough food to sustain him.

Once, a friend coming from Khurasan presented him with a fine, embellished and handsome gown, saying to him, "I've brought you this gown from Khurasan. I would be pleased to see you take off this rough gown and wear this nice one." Ibn Umar said, "Show it to me then." He touched it asking, "Is it silk?" His friend said, "No, it's cotton." Abdullah looked at it for a while then pushed it away with his right hand saying, "No, I'm afraid to tempt myself. I'm afraid it would turn me into an arrogant, proud man. Allah dislikes the arrogant, proud ones."

On another day, a friend presented him with a container filled with something. Ibn Umar asked him, "What's that?" He said, "Excellent medicine, which I brought you from Iraq!" Ibn Umar said, "What does it cure?" He said, "It digests food." Ibn Umar smiled and said to his friend, "Digests food? I haven't satisfied my appetite for 40 years."

He had not satisfied his appetite for 40 years not because of poverty, but rather due to self-denial and piety, in an attempt to imitate the Prophet ﷺ and his father. He was afraid to hear on the Day of Judgment: *You have wasted all your good deeds for the enjoyment in the life of this world* (46:20). He realised that he was in this life just as a visitor. He described himself thus: "I haven't put a stone upon another (i.e. I haven't built anything) nor planted a palm tree since the Prophet's death."

Maimun ibn Muhran once said, "I entered Ibn Umar's house and tried to evaluate all that was inside, such as the bed, the blanket, the mat and so on. Indeed, everything. I didn't find it worth even 100 dirhams." Again, he was not miserly; he was very generous. But this lifestyle was due to his disdain for luxury, and his commitment to sincerity.

Ibn Umar lived long enough to witness the Umayyad period, when money became abundant and land ownership spread. A luxurious life became prevalent in most dwellings, let alone the wealthier estates. Despite all that, Ibn Umar stayed firm like a rooted mountain. He refused to slip away from his path and abandon his simple lifestyle. If life with its pleasure and prosperity was mentioned, he simply said, "I've agreed with my companions upon a matter. I'm afraid if I change my stance, I won't meet them again." He was also known to have said, "O Allah, You know that if it weren't for fear of You, we would have emulated our clan in the Quraysh in this life."

Indeed, if it were not for his God-fearing nature, he would have rivalled people in their grandeur. But, he did not need to compete. Life continued to tempt him with its pleasures. For instance, is there any position more tempting than Caliph? It was offered to Ibn Umar several times, but he refused. Al Hasan reported that when Uthman ibn Affan was assassinated, they approached Abdullah ibn Umar saying, "You are the people's master and the son of the people's master. Go out so that people swear to you the oath of allegiance." He said, "By Allah, if I could, I would never allow a drop of blood to be shed because of me."

As time passed, civil strife became rampant and people often urged Ibn Umar to accept the position of Caliph. They were ready to swear to him the oath of allegiance, but he constantly refused. His reasoning was logical, because after the murder of Uthman the situation got much worse and took a dangerous turn.

Ibn Umar would have readily accepted the responsibilities and faced the dangers of being a Caliph, provided that he be voluntarily and willingly elected by all Muslims. However, he was opposed to the idea of forcing even one single Muslim to swear an oath of allegiance by the sword, and so he refused the post of Caliph altogether. At that time, this prospect would have been impossible. Despite his merits, and a general consensus of love and respect for him, other factors still made it impossible to reach any real agreement on the matter. For instance, the expansion of Islam into different regions, the long distances between those regions, and the in-fighting amongst the Muslims made his conditions unfeasible.

A man once met him and said, "No one is more evil in the whole Muslim community than you!" Ibn Umar said, "Why? By Allah, I've never shed their blood, or divided their community, or sowed dissension." The man replied, "If you had wished it, every single one would have agreed upon you." Ibn Umar said, "I don't like to see it (the caliphate) being offered to me while one man says no and another says yes."

The people still loved him even after the caliphate went to Muawiyah, then to his son Yazid, then to Muawiyah II, son of Yazid, who stepped down renouncing its pleasure after only a few days in office. Even on that day, when Ibn Umar was an old man, he was still the people's hope for the caliphate. Marwan went to him saying, "Give me your hand to swear the oath of allegiance. You're the master of the Arabs, and the son of their master." Ibn Umar asked, "What are we going to do with the people of the East?" Marwan said, "Beat them until they swear the oath." Ibn Umar replied, "I don't like to be 70 years old and a man gets killed because of me." Marwan went away saying in warning: "I can see civil strife boiling in its pots, and the kingdom after Abu Laila (i.e. Muawiyah ibn Yazid) will end up in the hands of the victorious".

———.◊.———

This refusal to use force is what made Ibn Umar hold a position of neutrality and isolation during the armed civil strife between Ali and Muawiyah. In regards to this discontent, he said these solemn words:

"*To the one who says, 'Come to prayer,' I will respond. And to the one who says, 'Come to success,' I will respond. But to the one who says, 'Come to kill your Muslim brother to take his money,' I will say, 'No'.*"

Whilst he remained neutral, it must be said that Ibn Umar never acted in a hypocritical way. If he saw wrongdoing, he spoke up. He often confronted Muawiyah at the height of his power, saying: "If there is only a tiny hair between me and the people, it won't be torn." Another time, he confronted the preacher Al-Hajaj when he claimed, "Ibn Az-Zubair has distorted the Book of Allah!" Hereupon Ibn Umar shouted in his face, "You are lying! You are lying! You are lying!" Al-Hajaj was at a loss for words. He promised Ibn Umar the worst punishment, but Ibn Umar waved his hand in Al-Hajaj's face and replied, "If you do what you just promised, there is no wonder about it, for you are a foolish imposed ruler."

Despite his bravery, he remained cautious until his last days, never playing a role in the armed civil strife and refusing to favour either party. Abu Al-Aliah Al Barra related: "I was once walking behind Ibn Umar without him realising it. I heard him saying to himself, 'They are holding their swords, raising them high, killing each other, and saying, 'O Ibn Umar, give us a hand!'?'" He was filled with sorrow and pain seeing Muslims blood shed by their own hands. As already mentioned, he would never even wake a sleeping Muslim. So, if he could have stopped the war and bloodshed he would have. But the events were just too powerful, so he kept to his home.

We discovered later though that his heart was with Ali, based on a narration of what he said in his last days: "I never felt sorry about something that I missed except that I didn't fight on the side of Ali against the unjust party." However, when he refused to fight with Imam Ali, it was not because he sought a safe position, but rather because he refused the whole concept of in-fighting entirely.

He clarified this when Nafi asked him, "O Abu Abdur Rahman, you are the son of Umar and the Companion of the Prophet ﷺ and you are who you are. What hinders you from that matter?" He meant fighting on Ali's side. So, he replied, "What hinders me is that Allah has forbidden us to shed the blood of another Muslim. Allah the Mighty and Powerful said: ... *and continue fighting them until there is no more persecutions and Allah's religion prevails* (2:193) and we did that. We fought the disbelievers until Allah's religion prevailed, but now, what is it we are fighting for? I fought when the idols were all over the Sacred House, from the corner to the door, until Allah cleared the land of the Arabs from it [idolatry]. Should I now fight those who say, 'There is no god but Allah'?" That was his logic, his argument, and conviction. Thus he did not abstain from taking part in battle in order to escape fighting, nor did he passively refuse to determine the outcome of the civil war. Rather, he refused to hold a sword in the face of a Muslim brother.

Abdullah ibn Umar lived long and witnessed the days in which life "opened its gates to the Muslims." Money became more abundant, high positions more available. All the while ambition and desires spread, but Ibn Umar's humility, piety and peace only flourished. He turned consistently towards Allah and lived according to his firm belief. Nothing whatsoever could affect his virtuous nature, already shaped and modelled by Islam during his formative years.

The nature of life changed quite rapidly at the beginning of the Umayyad period. Change was inevitable and markedly changed the ambition of both state and individual. In the midst of the many temptations of an era filled with pleasure and war booty, Ibn Umar stood strong with his merits, good character and ongoing spiritual progress.

He had gained all that he desired in life, including the positive influence of his father. So much so that his contemporaries described him as such: "Ibn Umar died while being like Umar in his merit."

Moreover, dazzled by the glitter of his merits, his contemporaries liked to compare him with his father Umar. They would say, "Umar lived in a time when [others like him] could be found, and Ibn Umar lived in a time when there was no one similar to him." It is an exaggeration, but of course a forgivable one because Ibn Umar was one of the few who deserved such a compliment. But as for Umar, no one can be directly compared to him.

In the year 73 AH, the ship of eternity hoisted its sail towards the next life, carrying with it the last representative from the early days of revelation: Abdullah ibn Umar ibn Al-Khattab.[1]

---

[1] The last Companion to pass away was Anas Ibn Malik who died in Al-Basra in the year 91 or 93 AH

(6)

SA'AD IBN ABI WAQQAS

The Lion's Claws

The Commander of the Faithful, Umar ibn Al-Khattab, once received troubling news. He received reports that the Persians had launched deceitful attacks against the Muslims at the Battle of Al-Jisr. That battle cost the Muslims 4,000 lives in one day alone. Moreover, the Iraqis soon followed by renouncing their allegiance and violating agreed covenants. Therefore, Umar decided to personally lead the Muslim troops in a decisive fight against Persia.

He set out accompanied by some of his companions, leaving Ali ibn Abu Talib behind to act as his deputy over Medina. However, he had hardly left Medina when some of his companions asked him to return. His companions, Abdur Rahman ibn Awf in particular, felt it was unwise to risk the Caliph's life in battle, when Islam was at such a pivotal point.

So, Umar paused his journey, ordered the Muslims to gather for a public consultation, and sent for Ali ibn Abi Talib to join them. After some deliberation, all present accepted Abdur Rahman ibn Awf's opinion. The assembly decided that Umar was to return to Medina and another Muslim leader be chosen to combat the Persians.

Umar agreed to their decision, then asked his companions, "Whom do you see fit to be sent to Iraq?" They thought silently for a while. Then Abdur Rahman ibn Awf shouted, "I have found him!" Umar said, "Who is it?" Abdur Rahman said, "The Lion's Claws: Sa'ad ibn Malik Az-Zuhari." The Muslims supported his choice. Umar then sent for Sa'ad ibn Malik Az-Zuhari, also known as Sa'ad ibn Abi Waqqas, and appointed him governor of Iraq and Commander of the Army.

Who was the 'Lion's Claws'? It was he who the Prophet ﷺ - whilst seated with his Companions - would greet cheerfully as, "My maternal uncle." Sa'ad's grandfather was Uhaib ibn Manaf, the paternal uncle of Amina, the mother of the Prophet ﷺ. He accepted Islam very young, at just 17 years old. When he talked about himself, he would say, "I witnessed a day in which I was third in Islam," so we know that he was one of the first few people to embrace Islam.

When the Prophet ﷺ spoke about the 'one God' and the new religion (even before using Dar Al-Arqam as a refuge for himself and his earliest Companions), Sa'ad ibn Abi Waqqas had already sworn the oath of allegiance to the Prophet ﷺ. Historical and biographical sources inform us that Abu Bakr's conversion was the catalyst for Sa'ad embracing Islam, he may have even spoken with and been convinced by him directly. Others who were influenced by Abu Bakr to convert included Uthman ibn Affan, Az-Zubair ibn Al-Awwam, Abdur Rahman ibn Awf and Talha ibn Ubaid Allah.

Sa'ad ibn Abi Waqqas had many noble qualities which he could be proud of. However, he never mentioned any of these merits himself, apart from two particular achievements which he cherished. Firstly, he was the first person to throw a spear in the cause of Allah and the also the first to be struck by one. Secondly, he was the only one for whom the Prophet ﷺ had prayed that his own parents be ransom. Ali ibn Abi Talib narrated about this: "I have never heard the Prophet ﷺ hoping that his parents may be made someone's ransom, except for Sa'ad. On the day of Uhud I heard the Prophet ﷺ say, "Throw, Sa'ad. May my father and mother be your ransom". So, of course, Sa'ad always proudly mentioned these two noble blessings.

Sa'ad was considered to be one of the most courageous horsemen amongst the Muslims, and indeed the Arabs. He possessed two weapons, his lance and his prayer. Whenever he pierced an enemy with his lance, he hurt him; whenever he invoked Allah, He answered. He and the Companions always saw that this was due to the Prophet's prayer in favour of him. One day, when the Prophet ﷺ saw Sa'ad doing something which delighted him, he made the following plea: "O Allah, make his spear hit unerringly and answer his prayer."

It was in this way that he became famous among his companions for his prayer, which was like a sharp sword when he wielded it. He knew that about himself; therefore, he was careful never to curse anyone. Sa'ad would just trust that Allah would do with them as He wished. An example of that is recorded by Amir ibn Sa'ad when he narrated that Sa'ad once saw a man insulting Ali, Talha and Az-Zubair. He forbade him, but he didn't stop. So Sa'ad said, "Then I will invoke Allah against you." The man said, "You're threatening me as if you were a Prophet".

Sa'ad went away, performed his ablution and prayed two rakahs. Then he lifted his hands up and said, "O Allah, if you know that that man has insulted people who have already been granted by you that which is the best, and his cursing of them has annoyed You, then make an example out of him." Only a short while had passed, when a stray camel went out of a house. Nothing could stop it till it entered a crowd as if searching for something. Then it attacked the man, and he fell between its legs. It continued to kick the man down till he died.

If this phenomenon was to prove something, it proved primarily the purity of Sa'ad's soul, the honesty of his faith, and the depth of his sincerity. He always sought to support his piety by ensuring he only consumed halal – both in food and in finance. And still, Sa'ad became one of the wealthiest Muslims around, leaving behind a great fortune after his death. It is rare that an abundance of money is acquired legitimately, but they certainly worked hand in hand for Sa'ad. And so, Allah granted him a great deal of halal money, which he also spent in the charitable endeavours. His ability to collect purely halal money was equal, if not second, to his ability to donate it in the cause of Allah.

He fell ill during the Farewell Pilgrimage, when he was accompanying the Prophet. Sa'ad asked him ﷺ, "O Messenger of Allah, I own a lot of money and there is nobody to inherit from me except one daughter. May I contribute two thirds of my money as alms?" The Prophet ﷺ said, "No." Then he said, "Then half of it?" The Prophet said, "No." Then he said, "Then a third?" The Prophet replied, "Yes, and the third is too much. To leave your heirs wealthy is better than to leave them having to be dependent on someone. If you spend any money in the cause of Allah, you'll be rewarded for it, even the morsel which you put in your wife's mouth."

Sa'ad did not actually remain the father of just one daughter, because he was later blessed with other children.

———·◦·———

Sa'ad would often cry out of sheer piety. Whenever he listened to the Prophet ﷺ preaching or advising, tears rolled down his face. Once, the Messenger was sitting with his Companions when his eyes gazed distractedly at the horizon. Then, he looked at his Companions' faces and said, "A man who belongs to Paradise will soon appear." The Companions turned in all directions trying to learn who this successful person might be. After a while, it was Sa'ad who appeared as predicted. So, later on, Abdullah ibn Amr ibn Al-As asked Sa'ad repeatedly to tell him the special worship or deed he had done which made him eligible for such a reward. Sa'ad told him, "Nothing more than what we all do or worship, except that I don't carry any spite or hatred towards any Muslim."

This was the 'Lion's Claws'. This was the man who Umar chose for the great day at the Battle of Al-Qadisiyah. The Commander of the Faithful had full insight into Sa'ad's many merits when he chose him for the difficult task of confronting the enemies of Islam and the Muslims. Umar observed the following:

- Sa'ad's prayers were heard and answered; if Sa'ad asked Allah for victory, he would be granted it.
- His food was pure, his tongue was pure, his conscience was pure.
- As the Messenger ﷺ had prophesied, Sa'ad was a man who belonged to Paradise.
- He was the horseman on the Day of Badr, the horseman on the Day of Uhud and in every battle he faced with the Prophet ﷺ.

Another thing, which Umar never underestimated, was the value of Sa'ad's firmness of faith. Umar had not forgotten what happened between Sa'ad and his mother when he converted to Islam. At that time, all attempts to obstruct him from Allah's cause had failed. His mother, therefore, used an approach which none doubted would conquer Sa'ad's soul and bring him back to his people's idols. She announced her abstention from food and drink until Sa'ad returned to his ancestral religion. She actually continued her hunger strike till she was near death.

Despite all that, Sa'ad refused to sell his faith. Hoping that his heart would yield upon seeing her, some relatives took Sa'ad to his mother. Sa'ad went to her and beheld her emotional plight. But, his belief in Allah and His Messenger ﷺ proved to be stronger than iron. He came near to her and shouted so that she could hear him, "You know, by Allah, mother, if you had 100 souls coming out one after the other, I wouldn't abandon my faith in return for anything. Then eat if you like, or don't eat!"

His mother changed her mind. A divine revelation greeted Sa'ad's position and supported it: *But if they (both) strive with you to make you join in worship with Me others that of which you have no knowledge, then obey them not...* (31:15).

So, was he not, indeed, the 'Lion' with his claws bared? That is why Umar handed him the standard of Al-Qadisiyah and unleashed him on the Persians. The Persian army had recruited more than 100,000 trained warriors. They were armed with particularly dangerous weapons, and led by the most cunning of warlords. Sa'ad, on the other hand, was not well prepared, with just 30,000 warriors, and equipped with only spears. However, the Muslim army's hearts were filled with the will of the new faith and all it represented: belief, vigour, and a rare aspiration for martyrdom.

As the two armies met in combat Sa'ad awaited the instructions of the Commander of the Faithful. Finally, Umar's message arrived, ordering him to move towards Al-Qadisiyah, the gate to Persia. Umar's words offered light and guidance: "O Sa'ad ibn Waqqas, do not be deluded if it is said, 'You are the Prophet's uncle and his Companion'. Know that there is no relationship between Allah and anyone except through obedience to Him. All people, the noble ones as well as the lowly, all are equal in front of Allah. Allah is their God and they are His servants. The relationship between them is one of rivalry for preference by means of their well-being, whereas they can only get what is in Allah's hands by means of obedience to Him. Remember the Prophet's ﷺ position, which he stuck to from the time he was sent to us until he left our world. Hold to them; it is an order."

Then he told him, "Send me information about your circumstances. Where have you reached and how? What is your enemy's position in respect to yours? Let your messages make me feel as if I am actually seeing you."

Sa'ad wrote to the Commander of the Faithful describing everything. He showed him practically each soldier's position. Sa'ad had reached Al-Qadisiyah. The Persians gathered their army as never before and appointed as their leader one of the most famous and dangerous commanders, Rustum. Sa'ad wrote to Umar to update him, and he replied: "Don't be upset by what you hear from them, nor what they show you. Seek Allah's help and put your trust in Him. Send them people of insight, good judgment, and patience to call him to follow Allah's path, and write to me every day."

Sa'ad wrote again to Umar saying, "Rustum camped with his troops at Sabat. He has brought his horses and elephants and marched towards us." Umar replied to calm him, complimenting Sa'ad as a smart, brave horseman, the Prophet's uncle, one of the first converts, and a hero of various wars. No sword or lance of Sa'ad's had ever failed to reach its target. He stood at the head of his army in one of the greatest historical battles as if he were an ordinary soldier, not deluded by power or acting arrogantly because of leadership. His self-esteem could have tempted him to rely only on his own capacities, but despite that he always turned to the Commander of the Faithful in Medina. Although miles separated them, he sent him a message each day to exchange viewpoints, advice, and opinions with the great battle still to come.

That was because Sa'ad knew that Umar also never made a decision alone, but consulted the Muslims and the Prophet's remaining Companions around him. Despite the war, Sa'ad did not want to deprive himself or his army of the benefits of public consultation, especially if Umar, a man with great inspiration, was among his consultants.

———•◊•———

Sa'ad carried out Umar's will and sent Rustum, the Persian leader, a number of his companions to call him to Islam. The conversation between them and the Persian leader lasted for some time. Finally, they ended their talk by telling him, "Allah has chosen us to turn whom He chooses of His creatures from paganism to monotheism, from the narrowness of life to its freedom, from ruler's injustice to Islam's fairness. Whoever accepts our offer, we will leave him alone and will refrain from hurting him. Whoever fights us, we will fight him until we fulfil Allah's promise."

Then Rustum asked, "What is Allah's promise which He made to you?" The Companion answered, "Paradise for our martyrs and victory for the living ones." The delegation returned to Sa'ad to tell him that it was war. Sa'ad's eyes filled with tears. He had wished so much that the war would be delayed for some time. On that day his illness became more severe, and he suffered its heavy burdens. Abscesses spread all over his body, to the extent that he could not sit, let alone ride his horse to take part in an extremely violent battle.

If the war had been waged just before his illness or had it been delayed till he was healthy again, then he would have proved himself brave. But this was his fate, and as the Messenger of Allah ﷺ had taught them, they should never say "if" because "if" shows weakness. A strong believer is neither helpless, nor weak. Thereupon the Lion's Claws stood up to preach to his soldiers. He began his speech citing the following glorious verse: *And We have written in the Zaboor (given to David) after the Torah (given to Moses): "My righteous servants shall inherit the earth* (21:105).

Having finished his speech Sa'ad led his troops in the Dhuhr Prayer, then turned towards his soldiers and proclaimed four times, "Allahu akbar (Allah is the Greatest)! Allahu akbar! Allahu akbar! Allahu akbar!" Then he stretched out his arm like an unerring arrow towards the enemy and proclaimed, "Let's start this battle, with Allah's blessings."

With pains hard to bear, he ascended to the balcony of his residence, which he used as a dwelling and a headquarter. On the balcony he sat on a pillow and leaned upon his chest. His door was left open, which meant that he was susceptible to even the slightest Persian attack, but he was far from afraid. His abscesses were bleeding and were extremely painful, but his mind was otherwise occupied. Sitting on his balcony, he was shouting, calling, and commanding. First to those in one flank to step forward towards the right, and then to those in another flank to fill out the empty spot on the left... "Mughirah, look forward! Jurair follow them! Numan, hit! Asharh, attack - and you also, Qaqa! Forward, forward, Prophet's Companions!"

His determined and hopeful voice turned each individual soldier into an army of their own. The Persian soldiers fell like flies and with them fell the worship of fire and paganism. After seeing the death of their commander and their best soldiers, the defeated, scattered remnants of Rustum's army fled. The Muslim army pursued them until they reached Nahawind, then Al-Al-Mada'in. There they fought till they carried home the emperor's throne and crown as war booty.

At the Battle of Al-Mada'in, Sa'ad's health had returned and he could prove his bravery once more. The Battle of Al-Mada'in took place two years after the Battle of Al-Qadisiyah. During that time, continuous armed clashes took place between the Muslims and the Persians. Finally, the scattered remnants of the Persian army gathered at Al-Mada'in, ready for a decisive and final battle. Sa'ad realised that time was on his enemy's side; therefore, he decided to deprive them of this advantage, but how? The Tigris River in its flood season stood in the middle between him and Al-Mada'in. Thereby, an event took place by which

Sa'ad succeeded to prove that he indeed deserved Abdur Rahman ibn Awf's description of him as the 'Lion's Claws'. Sa'ad's faith and determination stood stark in the face of danger, mocking the impossible with his unfailing bravery.

So, Sa'ad ordered his army to cross the Tigris River. He ordered them to search for a safe, secure ford in the river which would enable their crossing. Finally, they found a place, but the ford was not free of risk. Before the army started to cross, Sa'ad wisely recognised the need for safeguarding their landing spot on the opposite bank, where the enemy was camping. Therefore, he prepared two detachments, the first of which was called The Detachment of Terror. Its leader was Asim ibn Amr. The second was called The Detachment of the Dumb, led by Al Qaqa ibn Amr.

The soldiers of these two detachments had to face many difficult challenges in order to clear a safe space on the opposite bank for the army to land on. They fulfilled their task with exceptional skill. Sa'ad's success on that day surprised even him and continues to perplex historians. It also amazed his companion and escort Salman Al-Farsi, who shook his head in astonishment and said, "Islam is indeed new. By Allah, seas have been subdued by them and the land has been subdued by them. In the name of the One in Whose hands Salman's soul lies, they will leave it in a group, as they entered it in a group."

Indeed, that is exactly what happened. Just as they accessed the Tigris River in a group, so too did they leave it (in a group), without losing a single soldier. Some historical sources described the magnificence of such a scene as the fording of the river: Sa'ad ordered the Muslims to say, "Allah is enough for us and He is the best to trust in." Then he penetrated the Tigris with his horse, and the people followed behind him. No one stayed behind. They walked as if they were walking on land until they filled the whole area between the two banks. The surface of the water could not be seen because of the sheer number of cavalry and infantry. People were so secure in Allah's victory, promise and support that they carried on talking while walking into the water, as if they were walking on land.

———•◊•———

When Umar appointed Sa'ad to be Iraq's governor, he set out to build the city of Kufa and established the foundations of Islam throughout the land. One day though, the inhabitants of Kufa complained to the Commander of the Faithful about Sa'ad. They had lost control over their restless tempers and made the strange claim that, "Sa'ad can't pray well." Sa'ad laughed aloud and said, "By Allah, I prayed with them exactly as the Prophet's prayer was. I prolonged the first two rakahs and shortened the last two".

When Umar ordered him back to Medina, Sa'ad was not annoyed. On the contrary, he responded to Umar's call immediately. After some time, Umar decided to return him to Kufa, but Sa'ad responded laughing, "Do you order me to return to people who claim that I don't perform my prayers well?" He preferred to stay in Medina.

When Umar's life was under attack, he chose six of the Prophet's Companions to be responsible for choosing the next Caliph. Umar said that he chose six of those with whom the Prophet ﷺ was pleased before he died. Sa'ad ibn Abi Waqqas was one of them. But it seems from Umar's last words that if he would have chosen one of the Companions for the caliphate, it would have been Sa'ad. He said to his companions, advising and commending, "If Sa'ad is to become Caliph, that's good; but if someone else is to be Caliph, then he has to seek Sa'ad's help."

Sa'ad lived long. He secluded himself during the period of civil strife that followed the death of the third Caliph, Uthman. In fact, he ordered his whole family not to tell him any news about what was happening. Everyone was anxious to know his position on the civil unrest and once, his nephew Hashim ibn Utbah ibn Abi Waqqas, said to him, "O Uncle, here are 100,000 swords which considers your entitlement more favourably (i.e. the caliphate)." Sa'ad responded, "I want out of the 100,000 swords, just one sword that if it hits a believer it won't do anything, but if it hits a disbeliever it cuts through." His nephew realised what he meant and left him in his isolation and security.

When the dispute ended in favour of Muawiyah, who took over the reins of government, he asked Sa'ad, "Why didn't you fight with us?" He answered, "A dark cloud passed over me. I told it, Shoo! Shoo! I stopped my riding camel until it passed away."

Muawiyah said, "'Shoo! Shoo!' cannot be found in the glorious Book of Allah, but Allah said: *And if two parties or groups among the believers fall into fighting, then make peace between them both, but if one of them rebels against the other, then fight you (all) against the one that which rebels till it complies with the Command of Allah* (49:9). And you did not take anyone's side. You weren't with the unjust against the just, nor were you with the just against the unjust." Hereupon Sa'ad responded, "I wouldn't have fought a man (he meant Ali) to whom the Prophet ﷺ said, 'You have towards me the same position Harun (Aron) had towards Musa (Moses), except that there isn't any Prophet coming after me.'"

One day in 54 AH, having exceeded the age of 80, Sa'ad was at his house in Al-Aqiq preparing to meet Allah. His son spoke of his final moments: "His head was upon my lap; he was passing away. I cried, but he said, 'What makes you cry, my son? Allah will never torture me. I belong to Paradise!'" The firmness of his faith could not be weakened even by the quaking fear of death. The Prophet ﷺ had passed him the good news and he believed firmly in the Prophet's honesty; therefore, what was there to be afraid of?

However, he wanted to meet Allah carrying the most magnificent and most wonderful memory, a memory which joined him with his religion and his Prophet ﷺ. Therefore, he pointed to his coffer. They opened it and got out an old, torn, threadbare gown. He ordered his kin to shroud him in that gown saying, "I met the disbelievers at the Battle of Badr wearing it. I've saved it for this day."

Indeed, this threadbare gown was not just a gown. It was a banner waving over his long, great life. Our hero lived that life honestly, bravely, and faithfully. The body of the last Muhajirun was buried in Medina, safely laid beside a group of great Companions who preceded him to Allah. Their exhausted bodies had finally found a secure shelter in the ground of Al-Baqi cemetery.

Farewell Sa'ad, the hero of Al-Qadisiyah, conqueror of Al-Mada'in, extinguisher forever of the worshipped fire of Persia!

(7)

SUHAIB IBN SINAN

A Successful Purchase

Suhaib was born surrounded by comfort and luxury. His father was the governor of Al-Uballah (who acted as ruler on behalf of the Persian king), and he was also one of the Arabs who emigrated to Iraq long before Islam. In his palace on the bank of Euphrates, next to Mosul, the child lived happily and comfortably.

One day the country was attacked by the Romans (Byzantines) who captured a large number and enslaved the boy Suhaib ibn Sinan. He was taken by slave traders until finally his long journey ended in Makkah. There he was sold to Abdullah ibn Judan, after having spent most of his childhood in Roman lands, where he adopted their language and dialect. His master was so amazed by his intelligence, energy, and sincerity that he emancipated him, giving him the privilege of trading alongside him.

His friend Ammar ibn Yasir relates a story about what happened when Suhaib first met the Prophet ﷺ: "I met Suhaib ibn Sinan in front of the door of Dar Al-Arqam when the Prophet was there. I asked, 'What do you want?' He answered, 'And what do you want?' I said, 'I want to meet Muhammad to hear what he is saying.' He said, 'I want the same.' We both entered and met the Prophet ﷺ, who invited us to embrace Islam, and we converted. We stayed as we were till evening. He left secretly."

Thereupon, Suhaib got to know his path to Dar Al-Arqam. He got to know his path to guidance and light, but also to difficult sacrifice and great redemption. Entering through that wooden door, which separated Dar Al-Arqam and what was inside from the outer world, was not just crossing a threshold, but crossing of a whole world of limitations. An old world, with all that represented it — religion, manners, customs and life - crossing it towards a new world with all that represented it – a new set of religion, manners, customs, and life.

Crossing the threshold of Dar Al-Arqam, a threshold not wider than one foot, meant, in reality, to cross an ocean of terror. Stepping over such an obstacle meant the beginning of an era full of great responsibilities. As for the poor, the stranger, the enslaved, stepping over Dar Al-Arqam's threshold meant exceptional sacrifices. Suhaib, our hero, was such a stranger. Ammar ibn Yasir, his friend whom he met in front of the door, was a poor man. Why did they both go voluntarily to face this terror and, moreover, do their best when they met with it in combat?

It was the call of faith, which could not be resisted. It was the good character of Muhammad ﷺ, the scent of which filled the hearts of the reverent with love and guidance. These people were tired of the old misguidance and moral bankruptcy that surrounded them. And, above all, it was Allah's mercy that drew them to this new life, bestowed upon whomever He wishes; a guidance and protection bestowed on whomever turns to Him.

Suhaib holds a position in the ranks of the faithful. He held a high position among the persecuted, among the generous, and among the self-sacrificing. Suhaib once frankly described his loyalty to the Prophet ﷺ and Islam as follows: "I was present in every situation witnessed by the Prophet ﷺ. I was present at every pledge called by him. I was present in every detachment organised by him. The Prophet ﷺ never took part in a raid (at the beginning or at the end of a period), without my being on his right or left. Whenever the Muslims feared a danger facing them, I was there in the front, and whenever they feared it in the rear, I was there at the back. I never let the Prophet ﷺ stay in a position between me and the foe until he met Allah."

His words provide a dazzling account of his extraordinary faith and loyalty. Ever since the first day he received Allah's light and put his hand into the Prophet's, Suhaib (may Allah be pleased with him and with all his Companions) was imbued with such outstanding faith.

From that day, his relationship towards people and the world, let alone himself, acquired a new dimension. From that day, his character turned into a firm, humble and devoted one, braving every type of horror. He went on bravely and courageously shouldering his responsibilities, and never lagged behind whenever danger appeared. His desires were not directed towards gains and spoils of war, but rather towards sacrifice and ransom; not towards the greed of life but rather towards the passion of self- sacrifice.

He began the days of his noble redemption and great loyalty with the day of his hijra. On that day he abandoned all his wealth, all his gold which he had gained by successful trade during the long years he lived in Makkah. He abandoned all his fortune, all that he owned in a split second, the glory of which was never stained by doubt or retreat.

When the Prophet ﷺ intended to emigrate, Suhaib was supposed to be the third of the party: the Prophet, Abu Bakr, and Suhaib. However, the Quraysh decided to prevent the Prophet's emigration. Suhaib fell into one of their traps and was thereby hindered for some time from emigrating, while the Prophet ﷺ and Abu Bakr set out accompanied by Allah's blessing.

Suhaib disputed, talked, and argued until he got rid of his persecutors. He mounted his camel and sped across the desert. However, the Quraysh sent its hunters to follow him. When they reached him, Suhaib had hardly seen them before facing them and shouting from a near distance, "O people of Quraysh, you know that I am the best marksman. By Allah, you cannot reach me before I shoot each of my arrows with my bow, then I will strike you with my sword until it falls down. Come, if you'd like to try. Or if you like, I will tell you where my money is, and so leave me alone."

They agreed to take his money saying, "You came to us as a poor wretch. Your money increased in our land and among us you claimed high rank and now you want to escape together with your money?" He guided them to the place where he had hidden his fortune, then they left him alone and returned to Makkah.

Strangely enough, they believed his words without doubt, without precaution. They did not ask him to prove his honesty, nor did they ask him to swear, because they knew he was an honest and truthful man. Alone but happy, Suhaib continued his journey until he reached the Prophet ﷺ at Quba.

When Suhaib came into view, the Prophet ﷺ was sitting surrounded by his Companions. As soon as Muhammad ﷺ saw him, he called out his name cheerfully, "O Abu Yahia! A profitable sale! A profitable sale!" Hereupon, the glorious verse was revealed: *And of mankind is he who would sell himself, seeking the Pleasure of Allah (i.e a type of man who gives his life to earn the pleasure of Allah). And Allah is full of Kindness to (His) slaves.* (2:207)

Indeed, Suhaib had surrendered all his fortune — the fortune he accumulated during his entire youth — in return for his faithful soul. He never felt it was an unjust bargain. Money, gold, the whole world, nothing of that sort was worthwhile as long as he kept his faith, the sovereignty of his conscience, and the determination of his fate.

The Prophet ﷺ loved him very much. Besides being pious and God-fearing, he was a cheerful and jovial person. The Prophet saw him once eating dates when there was an inflammation in one of his eyes. He asked Suhaib jokingly, "Do you eat dates when there is inflammation in one of your eyes?" He answered, "What's wrong with that? I eat them with the other eye!"

He was a generous donor, spending all his stipend from the Bait Al-Mal in the cause of Allah - helping the needy, aiding the sorrowful, feeding the orphans and captives with the best of food. His extreme generosity once attracted the attention of Umar, who said to him, "I can see you feeding people too much, to the extent that you are spending lavishly." Suhaib answered him, "I've heard the Prophet ﷺ say, 'The best of you is the one who feeds (others).'"

Suhaib's life was filled with an abundance of merits and great situations. To be chosen by Umar ibn Al-Khattab to lead the prayer was yet another merit for his collection. When the Commander of the Faithful was attacked while leading the Muslims in the Fajr prayer and he felt his end was near, he began to advise his companions. Some of his last words were, "Let Suhaib lead people in prayer."

On that day Umar chose six of the Prophet's Companions and entrusted them with the choice of the new Caliph. The Caliph of the Muslims was always the one who led the prayers. In those days following the death of the Commander of the Faithful until the new Caliph was chosen, who was to lead the Muslims in prayer? He chose Suhaib. He chose him to lead the Muslims in prayer until the next Caliph came to carry out his duties. He chose him, despite the obvious Roman accent in his pronunciation. He chose him for his strength of faith and good character, and this choice was a divine blessing upon the pious worshipper Suhaib ibn Sinan.

(8)

MUAD IBN JABAL

An Expert in Halal and Haram

Among the 70 man delegation of the Ansar who swore the oath of allegiance to the Prophet ﷺ (in the Second Allegiance of Aqabah) sat a young man with a bright face, graceful eyes, and a radiant smile. When he was silent, he attracted attention with his profound peacefulness and devoutness. On the other hand, when he spoke, he held people spellbound. This young man was Muad ibn Jabal (may Allah be pleased with him). He belonged to the Ansar, and was among the foremost believers who gave the second oath of allegiance to the Prophet. He was renowned for his knowledge of fiqh (jurisprudence) - the practical aspect of Muhammad's message. He was so much of an expert in this field that the Prophet ﷺ once said of him, "The most learned man of my nation in halal and haram is Muad ibn Jabal."

He resembled Umar ibn Al-Khattab in his enlightenment, courage, and intelligence. When the Prophet sent him to Yemen, he asked him, "How will you give a judgment or settle a dispute?" Muad answered; "I will refer to the Quran." The Prophet then asked, "What will you do if you do not find the decree you are looking for in the Quran?" Muad answered, "I will refer to the Prophet's Sunnah." The Prophet then asked, "But what will you do if you do not find a decree even in the Sunnah?" Muad readily answered, "I will be judge between mankind by resorting to juristic reasoning (ijtihad) to the best of my power." This exchange shows us that Muad's staunch commitment to Allah's Book and the Prophet's Sunnah does not mean that he closed his mind to the countless considerations that await someone willing to perform ijtihad to unravel a matter.

Perhaps both Muad's ability in juristic reasoning, and the courageous usage of his intelligence enabled him to master the art of fiqh, excelling all other scholars. The Prophet ﷺ justifiably described Muad as "the most learned man of my nation in halal and haram." History portrays him as a man with a remarkably enlightened, resolute, and decisive mind. For instance, Ubayd Allah ibn Abdullah narrated that one day he entered the mosque with the Companions of the Prophet at the dawn of Umar's caliphate. Then he narrates: "I sat with a group of more than 30 men. They were recalling a hadith of the Prophet ﷺ. In this circle sat a dark, swarthy young man who had a sweet voice and a radiant face. Whenever they disputed about a hidden or ambiguous meaning in the hadith, they at once sought his legal instruction or judgment.

He seldom, if ever, spoke unless he was asked. When their meeting was over, I approached him and asked him, 'Who are you, O Allah's Slave?' He answered, 'I am Muad ibn Jabal'. So, I instantly felt close to him."

Also, Shahr ibn Hawshab said, "Whenever Muad ibn Jabal was present when the Companions of the Prophet were holding a meeting, they looked at him with reverence." Umar ibn Al-Khattab, the Commander of the Faithful, often consulted him. It seemed that Muad had a highly disciplined mind and a captivating and convincing logic. When we look at his historical background, we will always see him at the centre of attention. He always maintained a discrete silence in gatherings that was only broken whenever people were anxious to hear his judgment amidst a dispute. When he spoke, he looked (as one of his contemporaries described), "As if light and pearls were emanating from his mouth rather than speech." He reached his high rank in knowledge and reverence when the Prophet ﷺ was alive and maintained this status after his death, although Muad happened to die young, during Umar's caliphate, at the age of just 33 years.

During his life, Muad was generous, well-mannered, and good-natured. If anyone asked him for money, he would readily and gladly give it to him. His generosity made him spend all his money on charity and aid. When the Prophet ﷺ died, Muad was still in Yemen, where the Prophet had sent him with the task of teaching Muslims their religion and fiqh.

When Muad returned from Yemen during Abu Bakr's caliphate, Umar ibn Al Khattab was informed that Muad had become wealthy, and to purify that income he suggested to Abu Bakr that the community should have half of Muad's wealth. Umar rushed to Muad's house and told him about what he and Abu Bakr had agreed on. Muad was an honest and trustworthy man. The fact that he had made a fortune did not make him vulnerable to suspicion or sin; therefore, he turned down Umar's suggestion and refuted his viewpoint. Finally, Umar left him.

The next day, Muad hurried towards Umar's house and no sooner had he laid his eyes on him than he hugged him. His tears flowed as he said, "Last night, I saw in my dream that I was crossing deep water. I nearly drowned were it not for your help, Umar." Afterwards, they both went to Abu Bakr's presence where Muad asked him to take half of his money, but Abu Bakr said, "No, I will take nothing from you." Umar glanced at Muad and said, "Now it is halal and blessed."

What is interesting from this account is that Umar was not trying to accuse or cast suspicion on Muad, but the pious Abu Bakr also wanted to be absolutely positive that Muad had earned the wealth in a lawful and halal way before accepting any money. Ultimately, it reminds us that this was an era filled with people who were in perpetual competition to climb to the apex of human perfection. Some of them soared with their good deeds and others followed a middle course. Regardless, all of them were travellers on a caravan of goodness.

"The Prophet ﷺ said one day, "O Muad, by Allah I love you dearly, so do not forget to recite after every prayer, 'Allah help me in remembering You, in offering thanks to You, and in worshiping You properly'." Indeed, even the Prophet ﷺ supplicated Allah to help him to remember Him. Allah's Messenger emphasised this to remind people that authority belongs to Allah, He has the power over all, and there is no power or any might except with His permission. Muad definitely grasped this fact. He did his utmost to cherish and apply this as a fundamental basis in his life from that moment onwards.

One day, the Prophet ﷺ ran into him so he asked him, "How are you this morning Muad?" He answered, "This morning I woke up as a true believer." The Prophet said, "Every truth has its manifestations, so what are the manifestations of your true belief?" Muad readily answered, "I have never woken up without believing that I might die before nightfall. I have never slept without believing that I might die before the morning and have never taken a step without believing that I might die before taking the next. It always seems to me that I can see each nation humbled to its knees and each nation called to its record of deeds. It always seems to me that I can see the dwellers of Paradise, wherein are delights everlasting, and the dwellers of Hell, wherein they are in disgracing torment." The Prophet ﷺ remarked, "Now you know, so stick to the truth as long as you live." Indeed Muad had submitted himself and his destiny to Allah, for Allah was all that mattered to him. It was accurate when Ibn Masud described Muad as "a leader having all the good and righteous qualities, obedient to Allah...who worshipped none but Allah. We used to liken him to Ibrahim ﷺ."

Muad advocated knowledge and the remembrance of Allah. Moreover, he invited mankind to seek only useful and true knowledge saying, "I warn you against the deviation of wise men. You will know the truth when you see it, for it has a distinctive light!" He believed that worship was an end and a means to attain justice. One day a Muslim asked him, "Teach me." Muad asked him, "Will you obey me if I teach you?" The man answered, "I will not disobey you in anything." He said then, "Fast, then break your fast. Pray during the night, but you must get some sleep. Earn what is halal and what is rightfully yours, and do not earn sin. Die as a true Muslim. Finally, I warn you against the supplication of those who have been wronged or oppressed." He believed that education meant knowledge and practice; therefore, he said, "Learn whatever you like to learn, yet Allah will not make your learning worthwhile unless you practice what you have learned."

He believed that remembrance of Allah required the perpetual remembrance of His greatness, and also that you should account for your own deeds before Allah does so. Al-Aswad ibn Hilal reported, "As we were walking with Muad one day, he said, 'Let us sit down for a while to meditate Allah's blessings'" Perhaps the reason behind his habit of discrete silence was his ceaseless meditation and contemplation. Likewise, him telling the Prophet ﷺ that he never took a step without believing that he might die before taking the next, may have been due to his profound remembrance of Allah.

———•◊•———

Towards the end of his life, Muad emigrated to Syria, where he lived among its people and the expatriates as a teacher and a scholar of fiqh. When Abu Ubaidah, the governor of Syria and a close friend of Muad, died, Caliph Umar ibn Al- Khattab assigned Muad to take his place as a ruler. After only a few months of his rule, Muad was taken ill and soon died, humble and repentant to Allah.

In his final moments, Muad faintly uttered great words that revealed the great believer he was. He gazed up into the sky and humbly supplicated Allah, the Most Merciful, saying, "Allah I used to fear You, but now I implore You. Allah, You know that I did not devote my life to travel in the lands or to earn money or property but rather dedicated it to knowledge, faith and obedience, notwithstanding intense heat or hardships." He stretched his hand as if he were shaking death's hand and fell into a coma. His last words were, "O Death, welcome! You are a long-awaited beloved."

When Umar the second Caliph was asked before his death, "If you choose your successor now, we will give him our allegiance," he answered, "If Muad ibn Jabal were alive and I made him my successor to the caliphate, then I died and met Allah Who asked me, 'Whom did you assign to rule Muhammad's nation?' I would answer, 'I assigned Muad ibn Jabal to rule it after I heard the Prophet ﷺ say Muad ibn Jabal is the Imam of those who have knowledge of Judgment Day."

(9)

AL-MIQDAD IBN AMR

The First Muslim Cavalryman

Al-Miqdad's companions once said of him: "The first cavalryman to strive in the way of Allah was Al-Miqdad ibn Al-Aswad, our hero, and Al-Miqdad ibn Amr was one and the same person."

The story behind this was that Al-Miqdad ibn Amr was in alliance with a man called Al-Aswad ibn Abd Yaghuth, who actually adopted Al-Miqdad. Thus, he was called Al-Miqdad ibn Al-Aswad until the Quranic verse which abrogated this type of adoption was revealed. Thereafter, he restored his father's name, Amr Ibn Sa'ad and became known as Al-Miqdad ibn Amr. Al-Miqdad was the seventh of the seven men who announced their Islam openly and in public. Therefore, he had his share of the Quraysh's abuse and atrocities. He tolerated them with the courageousness and satisfaction of a devoted disciple.

When we examine Al-Miqdad's character, his attitude during the Battle of Badr first comes to mind. His honour there impressed all those who witnessed it and made each of them wish it were he who had adopted such an attitude. Abdullah ibn Masud, the Companion of Allah's Prophet ﷺ said, "I have seen Al-Miqdad (may Allah be pleased with him) maintain a firm attitude and I was overtaken by a vicarious feeling to be in his place. This feeling enveloped me to the extent that I wished more than anything in the world that it would come true."

Let us explain. The Day of Badr was a crucial one, as the Quraysh marched against the Muslims with all their might, stubborn persistence, and haughtiness in hand. On that day, the Muslims were not only few, but also untried and inexperienced in war. Their hearts had not been tested in action. The Battle of Badr was the dawn of their conquests. The Prophet ﷺ stood there to strengthen the faith of his Companions and test their combat-readiness to break through the enemy infantry and cavalry.

Afterwards, the Prophet ﷺ began to consult with his comrades on war tactics. Surely, the Prophet's Companions knew that when he asked their opinion, he demanded their personal and courageous opinion, even if it happened to contradict the majority. He who expressed his opinion would not be reproached or criticised.

Al-Miqdad was afraid of speaking, lest one of the Muslims should have reservations about the imminent battle. So, before he had the chance to open his mouth, Abu Bakr Al-Siddiq started talking. By the time he had finished his words however, Al-Miqdad's apprehensions had all but vanished, for Abu Bakr spoke with remarkable eloquence. Umar ibn Al-Khattab spoke next and followed suit. Finally, Al-Miqdad stepped forward and said, "O Prophet of Allah, go ahead with what Allah has inspired you to do. We will stand by you. By Allah, we will never say as the Children of Israel said, 'So go you and your Lord and do battle, we are sitting right here.' Instead, we will say, 'Go you and your Lord and we will fight with you.' By Allah, Who has sent you with the truth, if you take us to the end of the world, we will tolerate all hardships until we reach it with you. We will fight on your left, your right, in front of you and behind you until Allah bestows victory on you." His decisive words made his righteous compatriots fill with enthusiasm.

The Prophet's face brightened as he uttered a special supplication for Al-Miqdad, whose words were so decisive that they drew a pattern for others to follow when speaking after. Indeed, Al-Miqdad's words left their impact on the hearts of the believers. Consequently, Sa'ad ibn Muad, a leader of the Ansar, rose and said, "O Prophet of Allah, we have believed in you and witnessed that what has descended on you is the truth. We gave you our allegiance, so go ahead with what you intend to do, and we will stand by you. By Allah Who has sent you with the truth, if you attempt to cross the sea, we will cross it hand in hand with you. None of us will lag behind or turn his back on you. We are not afraid to meet our enemy tomorrow, for we are experienced in war, capable of fighting and we are faithful in our desire to meet Allah. I pray to Allah that we do what will make you proud of us. Go ahead with Allah's blessings."

The Prophet ﷺ felt sanguine on hearing this, and said to his Companions, "March forward, and be cheerful and confident!" After a while the two armies met in fierce combat. The Muslim cavalry on that day were only three: Al-Miqdad ibn Amr, Marthad ibn Abi Marthad, and Az-Zubair ibn Al-Awam. The rest of the Mujahidun were either infantry or riding on camels, but still the Muslims prospered in battle.

Al-Miqdad was a wise and intelligent man. His wisdom was not expressed in just words, but in his consistent conduct. His experience was the fuel of his wisdom and intelligence. The Prophet ﷺ once assigned him to rule one of the governorships, and when he returned the Prophet asked him, "How does it feel to be a governor?" He answered with admirable honesty: "It made me feel as if I were in a silver tower above the rest of the people. By Allah Who has sent you with the truth, from now on, I will never expose myself to the temptations of governing."

This was an honest and straightforward man who was able to detect and admit his innermost weaknesses. His position as a governor made him vulnerable to arrogance and vain glory. He detected this fault in himself at once, and took a solemn oath to avoid any position that might jeopardise his righteousness. He kept his oath and renounced any influential or controversial position for the rest of his life. Al-Miqdad cherished the hadith of the Prophet ﷺ that says, "He who avoids fitna (trials, afflictions, and error) is indeed a happy man." He realised that because the governorship awakened a latent pride in him, it was better to avoid any such position altogether.

His wisdom often meant that he reserved judgment of others. This was also a trait that Allah's Prophet ﷺ instilled in him, for he taught Muslims that the hearts of the children of Adam are incredibly fickle. As such, Al-Miqdad would always try to delay his final judgment of a man until the moment of that man's death. This allowed him to be absolutely certain that the man in question had not changed path in the face of death.

Al-Miqdad's wisdom is particularly noticeable in the following exchange, narrated by one of his companions: "One day, we sat with Al-Miqdad, a man passed by and addressed Al-Miqdad saying, 'All kinds of happiness are for the eyes which have seen Allah's Prophet ﷺ. By Allah, we wish that we saw what you have seen and witnessed what you have witnessed'. Al-Miqdad approached him and said, 'Why should anyone wish to witness a scene that Allah did not wish him to see? He does not know what it would have been like if he had witnessed it or which side he would have been among if he went back in time. By Allah, Allah's Prophet ﷺ saw people who were thrown right into hell, so you should thank Allah that you were spared such a trial and are honoured by firm belief in Allah and His Prophet ﷺ'."

This was a remarkable kind of wisdom. You hardly ever meet a believer who loves Allah and the Prophet ﷺ, but who does not wish to see or live with him. And yet, Al-Miqadad's keen insight adds a missing dimension to this wish. For is it not possible that if this man had lived during those times, he might have ended up among the dwellers of Hell? Is it not possible that he might have sided with the disbelievers? Again, is it not far better for him to thank Allah who destined him to live at a time when Islam had become deeply-rooted? Al-Miqdad's viewpoint was both wise and intelligent.

His love for Islam was not only great, but also tempered with reason. Al-Miqdad's love for the Prophet ﷺ filled his heart and deepened his feeling of responsibility towards the Prophet's safety. No sooner was a call for an expedition announced, than he darted to the Prophet's house, sword in hand. His love for Islam filled his heart with a need to protect it, not only from the plots of its enemies, but also from the mistakes of its allies.

One day, his army unit was on an expedition, when the enemy troops managed to besiege them. Their commander therefore ordered his soldiers not to graze their camels. One of the Muslim soldiers did not hear this order and unintentionally disobeyed it. The commander punished him severely, more than he actually deserved (if he deserved to be punished at all). Al-Miqdad passed by this man and, finding him in tears, he asked him what was the matter. On discovering what had happened, Al-Miqdad took the man to the commander, where they argued until the commander was convinced of his error of judgment.

Then Al-Miqdad said, "Now it is the time for retaliation. He must have his qisas (the law of equity)." The commander accepted, but the soldier chose not to retaliate. Al-Miqdad was in awe of this act of forgiveness and felt the greatness of their religion that fostered such mercy. He said in praise, "I will see Islam triumphant, even if I have to die for it." Indeed, it was his extraordinary efforts to make Islam powerful before his death that made the Prophet ﷺ say to him, "O Al-Miqdad, Allah ordered me to love you and told me that He loves you."

(10)

SA'ID IBN AMIR

Greatness under Tattered Garments

Most of us will never have heard of Sa'id ibn Amir before. In short, Sa'id was one of the most outstanding, pious Companions of the Prophet ﷺ, despite the fact that his name is seldom, if ever, mentioned. Like all the able-bodied Muslims of that time, he would accompany the Prophet ﷺ in all his expeditions and battles. As a believer, he could never turn his back on Allah's Prophet, neither in war, nor in peace time.

Shortly before the Conquest of Khaibar, Sa'id submitted himself to Islam. Ever since he embraced Islam and gave his allegiance to the Prophet ﷺ, he dedicated his life to the service of the religion. All the great virtues of obedience, asceticism, dignity and piety combined seamlessly inside this kind man's character.

In our attempt to unveil his greatness, we must bear in mind that, in most cases, appearance contrasts with reality. If we judged him by his outer looks, we would not do him justice. He had dusty uncombed hair; nothing in his appearance distinguished him from poorest of Muslims and he did not seem impressive. But, if we delve into his inner self, we will see greatness in the true sense of the word. This greatness stood aloof from the splendour and ornament of life. Yet, it lurked there beyond his modest appearance and worn-out garments.

When the Commander of the Faithful, Umar ibn Al-Khattab, dismissed Muawiyah from his position as governor of Homs in Syria, he searched desperately for a qualified replacement. Umar's standards for governors were high, and as such his methods were cautious, meticulous, and thorough. He believed that if a governor in his employ committed a sin or error, two people would be asked to account for it before Allah: both Umar and the governor. His standards of evaluation were highly perceptive.

Centuries before the advent of Islam, Homs, was a big city that witnessed the dawn and eclipse of many civilisations. It was also a vital centre of trade, and the attractions of the city turned it into a place of seduction and temptation. In Umar's opinion, only a truly devout and repentant worshipper would be able to resist its attractions. Umar cried out when he realised: "Sa'id ibn Amir is the right man for this mission." He summoned him immediately.

Sa'id was offered the governorship by the Commander of the Faithful, but he refused saying, "Do not expose me to fitna." Umar then said, "By Allah, I will not let you turn me down. Do you lay the burdens of your trusteeship and the caliphate upon my shoulders, but then refuse to help me out?" Instantly, Sa'id was convinced of the logic of Umar's words. Indeed, it was not fair to abandon or avoid their obligation towards the caliphate. Moreover, if people like Sa'id ibn Amir renounced their responsibilities, then Umar would definitely struggle to find a man who was pious and righteous enough to be entrusted with such a mission.

Therefore, Sa'id agreed and travelled with his wife to Syria. They were newlywed. Ever since his bride was young, she had been an exquisite beauty. Umar gave him a considerable sum of money at the time of his departure. When they settled down in Syria, his wife wanted to use this money, so she asked him to buy appropriate garments, upholstery, and furniture for them, and to save the rest of it. Sa'id responded, "I have a better idea. We are in a country with profitable trade and brisk markets, so it would be better to give this money to a merchant so as to invest it." She said, "But what if he loses it?" Sa'id answered, "I will make him a guarantee that the amount will be paid." She agreed.

Sa'id, of course, went out and bought the necessities for an ascetic life; he then voluntarily gave all his remaining money to charity, for the poor and those in need. Time went by, and every now and then his wife would ask him about their money and their profits and he would answer, "It is a highly profitable trade."

One day, she asked him the same question before one of his relatives who knew what he had done with the money. His relative smiled, and he could not help laughing in a way that made Sa'id's wife suspicious. Therefore, she prevailed on him to tell her the truth. He told her, "Sa'id on that day gave all his money in voluntary charity in Allah's cause." Sa'id's wife was broken-hearted, for not only had she lost her last chance to buy what she wanted but also lost all their money.

Sa'id gazed at her sad eyes, wet with tears. Her sadness only added more to her charm, but before he forgot himself, he imagined Paradise inhabited by his late friends. He then Sa'id, "I had companions who preceded me in ascending to Allah, and you will not deviate me from the path they have taken, not for the world." His wife was accepting, for she realised that she had no choice but to follow Sa'id's example and

Allah, I hate to say the reason, but you force me to. Anyway, I have devoted the day to them and consecrated the night for Allah. As for the third complaint that they do not see me two days per month, well, I do not have a servant to wash my garment and I have no spare one. Therefore, I wash it and wait for it to dry shortly before sunset, then I go out of my house to meet them.

'My defence against the last complaint of the fainting fits is that I saw with my own eyes Khubaib Al-Ansari being slain in Makkah. The Quraysh cut his body into small pieces and said, 'Do you want to save yourself and see Muhammad in your place instead?' He answered, 'By Allah, I will not accept your offer of setting me free to return to my family safe and sound - even if you gave me all the splendours and ornaments of life in return for exposing the Prophet ﷺ to the least annoyance, that is if it was to prick a thorn.' Now, every time this scene of me standing there as a disbeliever, watching Khubaib being tortured to death and doing nothing to save him flickers in my mind, I find myself shaking with fear of Allah's punishment and I faint."

These were Sa'id's words as his tears flowed. The overjoyed Umar could not help but cry out, "All praises and thanks be to Allah Who would not make me disappointed in you!" He hugged Sa'id and kissed his graceful and dignified forehead.

———————◦———————

What a great guidance must have been bestowed on those outstanding men! What an excellent instructor Allah's Prophet ﷺ must have been! And, what a penetrating light emanated from Allah's Book! Sa'id ibn Amir was truly among the best of the early Muslims. His position allowed him a considerable salary, yet he took only enough money to buy the necessities for himself and his wife, and gave the rest in voluntary charity in the way of Allah. One day, he was urged to spend this surplus on his family and relatives, yet he answered, "Why should I give it to my family and relatives? No, by Allah, I will not sell Allah's pleasure to seek my kinfolks' pleasure."

He was later urged, "Spend more money on yourself and on your family and try to enjoy the lawful good things." But he always answered, "I will not stay behind the foremost Muslims after I heard the adapt herself to his rigid, ascetic, and pious way of life.

———————•◦•———————

At that time, Homs was nicknamed 'the second Kufa'. The [reason be]hind this was that its people were easily stirred and swayed against their governors. And so, Homs was named after the [Kufa,] which was also notorious for its endless uprisings. Although, [the people] of Homs were inclined towards rebellion, Allah guided thei[r hearts to] His righteous slave, Sa'id. They loved and obeyed him. One [day, Umar] said to Sa'id, "I find it rather strange that the people of Syri[a love and] obey you." Sa'id answered, "Maybe they love me because [I help and] sympathise with them."

Despite the people's love for Sa'id, their innate rebellio[us nature got] the better of them. Hence, murmurs of discontent began to [be heard.] One day, as the Commander of the Faithful was visiting [Homs, he] asked its people who gathered around him for their opinio[n of Sa'id.] Some made complaints against him which were in fact a [blessing in] disguise, for they unveiled the traits of an impressive man.

Umar asked the criticising group to state their complai[nts one by] one. The representative of the group stood up and said, "We [have four] complaints against Sa'id: First, he doesn't come out of his h[ouse until] the sun rises high and the day becomes hot. Second, he do[es not meet] anyone at night. Third, there are two days in every month in [which he] doesn't leave his house at all. Fourth, he faints every now and [then, and] this annoys us although he can't help it." The man sat down [and Umar] was silent for a while, whilst he privately supplicated to All[ah, saying,] "Allah, I know that he is one of Your best slaves. Allah, I be[g You] not to make me disappointed in him."

Umar summoned Sa'id to defend himself. Sa'id replied, "A[s for their] complaint that I do not get out of my house before noon, [in truth] I hate to explain the reason that made me do that, but I h[ave to do] so. The reason is that my wife does not have a servant, so I [knead the] dough, wait for it to rise, bake my bread, perform ablution[s, pray] Salat al-Duha, then I go out of my house." Umar's face bri[ghtened as] he said, "All praises and thanks be to Allah.'"

Then he urged Sa'id to refute the rest of the allegations. [Sa'id went] on, "As for their complaint that I do not meet anyone at [night,

Prophet ﷺ say, 'When Almighty Allah gathers all people on the Day of Reckoning, the poor believers will step forward in solemn procession. They will be asked to stop for reckoning but they will answer confidently: We have nothing to account for. Allah will say: My slaves said the truth. Hence, they will enter Paradise before all other people.' "

In 20 AH, Sa'id returned to Allah, with a pious heart and an honourable legacy. He yearned for so long to be among the foremost Muslims, so much so that he decided to fulfil their covenant and follow in their footsteps. He had yearned so long for his Prophet ﷺ and his beloved comrades; and he was finally able to leave all the burdens and hardships of life behind.

Peace be upon Sa'id ibn Amir. Peace be upon his life and resurrection. Peace be upon the honourable and obedient Companion of the Prophet ﷺ.

(11)

HAMZA IBN
ABDUL MUTTALIB

The Lion of Allah

After a day full of work, worship, and entertainment, the people of Makkah would always fall into a deep sleep. The people of the Quraysh were turning in their beds, except for one who had forsaken his sleep. He would always go to bed early, rest for a few hours, then wake up anxiously for his appointment with Allah. He went to pray in a corner of his room, and supplicate to his God. Whenever his wife woke upon hearing his long supplications, she shed tears of sympathy, asked him not to be so hard on himself, and told him to get some sleep. He only answered earnestly, "The time for sleep is over, Khadija."

At that time Muhammad ﷺ was not yet a serious problem for the Quraysh. Although he had started to draw their attention (as he had begun spreading his call in secret), those who believed in him were still only a few in number. There were people among the non-believers who loved and respected him. They yearned to declare their belief in him and become one of his followers, but their fear of the prevailing norms and the pressure of inherited traditions prevented them. Among them was Hamza ibn Abdul Muttalib, the Prophet's paternal uncle and foster brother (they had been breastfed by the same wet nurse).

---·◇·---

Hamza was fully aware of the greatness of his nephew and of the truth he came with. He used to know him not only as a nephew, but also as a brother and friend because they both belonged to the same generation. As children, they always played together, walking on the same road in life, side by side. But in their youth they parted ways: Hamza preferred the life of leisure, trying to take his place among the prominent leaders of the Quraysh; while Muhammad chose the life of seclusion away from the crowd, immersed in the deep spiritual meditation that ultimately prepared him to receive the revelation.

Despite the fact that each of them had a different way of living their youth, Hamza was always attentive to the virtues of his friend and nephew. Such virtues helped Muhammad to win a special place in the hearts of people and helped to draw a clear outline for his great future.

One day, Hamza went out as usual. At the Kaba he found a number of Quraysh's noblemen. He sat with them, listening to what they had to say - they were talking about Muhammad ﷺ. For the first time, Hamza saw them worried about his nephew's call. He noted their bitter tone and the rage in their voices. Before that, they had never paid attention (or at least they had pretended not to do so), but on that day their faces looked perplexed, upset, and aggressive.

Hamza laughed at their discussion and accused them of exaggeration. Abu Jahl said to his companions that Hamza was pretending to underestimate the danger. He warned that the Quraysh would relax too much, and soon Muhammad would have complete control over them all. And so, they kept talking and threatening whilst Hamza sat watching on, sometimes smiling, sometimes frowning. When they dispersed, his head was full of new ideas about the issues that they had discussed concerning his nephew.

Days passed and the Quraysh's whisperings about the Prophet's call only increased. Soon, that whispering turned into provocation, and Hamza watched the exchanges from a distance. His nephew's composed, steadfast attitude towards their taunting puzzled him. Such an attitude was quite unfamiliar to the Banu Quraysh, who were known to be challenging.

Hamza never doubted the greatness and truth of Muhammad ﷺ, because he knew Muhammad best - from his early childhood, to his proud and honest manhood. Hamza knew the Prophet as he knew himself, and maybe more. Since they had grown up together, and reached maturity side by side, Muhammad's life had always been as pure as light. It never seemed possible to Hamza that Muhammad ﷺ could make an error or commit a doubtful act. He never saw Muhammad angry, hopeless, greedy, careless or unstable.

Hamza was not only physically strong, but also wise and strong-willed. Therefore, it was natural for him to follow a man in whose honesty and truthfulness, he wholeheartedly believed. Thus, he kept a secret in his heart that would soon be disclosed.

The day finally arrived. Hamza set out from his house towards the desert, carrying his bow to practice his favourite pastime of hunting (in which he was very skilled). He spent most of his day there. On his way home, he passed by the Kaba as usual, to circumambulate it. Near the Kaba, a female servant of Abdullah ibn Judan saw him and said, "O Abu Umara! You haven't seen what happened to your nephew at the hands of Abu Al-Hakam ibn Hisham. When he saw Muhammad sitting there, he hurt him and called him bad names and treated him in a way that he hated." She went on to explain what Abu Jahl had done to the Prophet of Allah ﷺ.

Hamza listened to her carefully and paused for a while, then with his right hand he picked up his bow and put it on his shoulder. He walked with fast, steady steps towards the Kaba, hoping to meet Abu Jahl there. He decided that if he did not find him, he would search for him everywhere till he did.

As soon as he reached the Kaba, he glanced at Abu Jahl sitting in the yard in the middle of other noblemen. Hamza advanced very calmly towards Abu Jahl and hit him with his bow on the head till it broke the skin and bled. To everybody's surprise, Hamza shouted, "How dare you insult Muhammad while I follow his religion and I say what he says? Come and retaliate. Hit me if you can." In a moment they all forgot how their leader Abu Jahl had been insulted and they were all thunderstruck by the news that Hamza had converted to Muhammad's religion; that he saw what Muhammad saw, and said what he said. Could Hamza really have converted to Islam when he was the strongest and most dignified, young Quraysh man?

The Quraysh were helpless to such overwhelming news, because Hamza's conversion was sure to attract others from the elite to do the same. Muhammad's call was now garnering support, and he would find enough one day that the Quraysh might wake to find their idols pulled down.

———•◦•———

Again, Hamza picked up his bow and put it on his shoulder. With steady steps, he left everyone disappointed and Abu Jahl licking his wounds. He went home, and after he had relaxed from the day's exhaustion, he sat down to think over what had happened. He had announced his conversion in a moment of indignation and rage. He hated to see his nephew getting insulted and suffering injustice with no one to help him. Such zeal to protect the honour of Banu Hashim had made him hit Abu Jahl on the head and shout his declaration of Islam. But was that the ideal way for anyone to change the religion of his parents and ancestors? Was this the way to embrace a new religion, whose teachings he had not yet become familiar with, and whose true reality he had not acquired sufficient knowledge of? It was true that Hamza had never had any doubts about Muhammad's integrity, but could anybody embrace a new religion with all its responsibilities, in a moment of rage as Hamza had done?

It was true that he had always respected his nephew's call, but what should the right time have been to embrace this religion, if he was destined to embrace it? Should it have been a moment of anger, or a moment of deep reflection? Thus, he was inspired to reconsider the whole situation with a clear head, and to reflect closely on the matter.

Hamza started thinking. He spent many restless days and sleepless nights doing so. When one tries to attain the truth by the power of mind, uncertainty becomes a means of knowledge, and this is what happened to Hamza. Once he started considering Islam and weighing between the old religion and the new, he began to have doubts. These doubts were raised by his innate, inherited nostalgia for his father's religion, and by the natural fear of anything new. All his memories of the Kaba, the idols, and the high religious status these idols bestowed on the Quraysh and Makkah resurfaced.

It appeared to him that denying all this history and his ancient religion was suddenly a wide chasm to be crossed. Hamza was amazed at how a man could depart from the religion of his father so early and so fast. He regretted what he had done, but he went on with his journey of reflection. But at that moment, he realised that his mind was not strong enough and that he should resort sincerely to the unseen power. So, at the Kaba he prayed and supplicated to the heavens, seeking help from every light that existed in the universe to be guided to the right path.

Let us hear him narrating his own story: "I regretted having departed from the religion of my father and kin, and I was in terrible state of uncertainty and could not sleep. I came to the Kaba and supplicated to Allah to open my heart to what was right and to eliminate all doubts from it. Allah answered my prayer and filled my heart with faith and certainty. In the morning I went to the Prophet ﷺ informing him about myself, and he prayed to Allah that He may keep my heart stable in this religion."

This is how Hamza converted to Islam, the religion of certainty.

———⋄———

Allah boosted Islam with Hamza's conversion. Hamza was strong in his defence of both the Prophet ﷺ, and the helpless amongst his Companions. When Abu Jahl saw him among the Muslims, he realised that war was inevitable. Therefore, he began to support the Quraysh in their attempts to ruin the Prophet and his Companions. He wanted to prepare for a civil war to relieve his heart of his anger and bitter feelings.

Hamza was unable, of course, to prevent all the harm alone, but his conversion was a shield that protected the Muslims, and was the first source of attraction to many tribes to embrace Islam. The second source was Umar ibn Al-Khattab's conversion, after which people entered Allah's religion in crowds. Since his conversion, Hamza devoted all his life and power to Allah and His religion till the Prophet ﷺ honoured him with the noble title, "The Lion of Allah and of His Messenger".

The first military raid launched by the Muslims against their enemies was under the command of Hamza. The first banner that the Prophet handed to any Muslim was to Hamza. In the battle of Badr, when the two conflicting parties met, the Lion of Allah and of His Messenger were there to perform great feats in battle.

After Badr, the defeated remnants of the Quraysh army stumbled back to Makkah in disappointment. Abu Sufyan was utterly defeated as he left the dead bodies of the Quraysh 'martyrs' on the battlefield - such as Abu Jahl, Utbah ibn Rabia, Shaibah ibn Rabia, Umaiyah ibn Khalaf, Uqbah ibn Abi Muait, Al-Aswad ibn Abdul Asad Al-Makhzumi, Al-Walid ibn Utbah, Al-Nafr ibn Al-Harith, Al-As ibn Sa'id, Tamah ibn Addi, and scores of others.

But the Quraysh would not accept the defeat so easily. They started to prepare the army again and form alliances to avenge their honour and their dead. They insisted to continue the war. So, in the Battle of Uhud, the Quraysh battled alongside their Arab allies, under the leadership of Abu Sufyan once more.

The Quraysh leaders targeted two people in this battle, namely, the Prophet ﷺ and Hamza (may Allah be pleased with him). Before they went to war, they had already chosen the person in charge of assassinating Hamza: an Abyssinian slave with extraordinary skill in spear throwing. They planned for him to kill Hamza, his only role in the battle being to hit him with a deadly spear. They warned him not to be busy with any other preoccupation other than his target Hamza, regardless of the situation on the battlefield. They promised him the excellent reward of his freedom. The slave, whose name was Wahshi, was owned by Jubair ibn Mutam. Jubair's uncle had been killed in the Battle of Badr, so Jubair said to Wahshi, "Go out with the army, and if you kill Hamza you will be free."

After this offer, the Quraysh sent Wahshi to Hind bint Utbah, Abu Sufyan's wife, to give him more encouragement to kill Hamza. Hind had lost her father, uncle, brother, and son to the battle with the Muslims, and it was said that Hamza had been behind their deaths. This was the reason why Hind was the most enthusiastic one of all the Quraysh to escalate the war. All she wanted was Hamza's head, whatever the cost might be. She spent days before the battle pouring all her rage into Wahshi's heart and forging a plan for him. She promised him that if he killed Hamza, she would give him her most precious trinkets. With her hateful fingers she held her precious pearl earrings and a number of golden necklaces around her neck and gazed at him saying, "All these are yours if you kill Hamza." Wahshi's mouth watered at the offer, and his soul yearned for the battle to earn his freedom and Hind's prized possessions. It was clear then that this war sought Hamza's blood.

The Battle of Uhud began and the two armies met. Hamza stood in the middle of the battlefield dressed in his armour, an ostrich feather adorning his breast (as was customary for him in battle). He moved swiftly and adeptly around, slaying each polytheist he found in the Quraysh army. It seemed as if death was at his command.

The Muslims were on the verge of victory and the defeated army of the Quraysh started to withdraw in fright. But, just then the Muslim archers ignored commands and left their position on the mountain to collect the spoils of war left behind by the retreating Quraysh. Had they stayed in position, the battle would have been an enormous loss for the Quraysh, but in seeing an opening in the Muslim army, the Quraysh cavalry returned.

They attacked the Muslims by surprise from the back and struck at them with thirsty swords. The Muslims tried to pull themselves together, picking up the weapons they had put down, but the attack was too violent. When Hamza saw what had happened, he doubled his strength to retaliate. Hamza was striking all around him as Wahshi stood watching, waiting for the right moment. Let us hear Wahshi himself describe the scene:

"*I was an Abyssinian man who used to throw the spear in an Abyssinian way - a way that scarcely misses its target. When the armies met, I searched for Hamza till I found him in the middle of the crowd like a huge camel. He was killing everyone around him with his sword. Nothing could stop him. By Allah, I prepared for him. I wanted him. I hid behind a tree so that I might attack him or he might come close to me. At that moment Siba'a ibn Abdul Uzza approached him before me. When Hamza glanced at him he shouted, 'Come to me, you son of the one who circumcises!' and he hit him directly in the head. Then I shook my spear till I was in full control over it and threw it. The spear penetrated him from the back and came out from between his legs. He rose to reach me but could not and soon died. I came to his body and took my spear and went back to sit in the camp. I didn't want anything else to do with him. I killed him only to be free.*"

Wahshi goes on to describe his later conversion to Islam and interactions with the Prophet: "*When I returned to Makkah, they set me free. I stayed there till the Prophet ﷺ entered Makkah on the Day of the Conquest. I fled to Taif. When the delegation of Taif went to declare their conversion to Islam, I heard various people say that I should go to Syria or Yemen or any other place. While I was in such distress, a man said to me, 'Woe to you! The Prophet ﷺ never kills anyone entering his religion.' I went to Allah's Prophet ﷺ in Medina, and the moment he first saw me I was already giving my true testimony. When he saw me, he said, 'Is it you, Wahshi?' I said, 'Yes, Messenger of Allah.' He said, 'Tell me, how did you kill Hamza?' I told him, and when I finished he told me, 'Woe to you! Get out of my sight and never show your face to me.' From that time, I always avoided wherever the Prophet ﷺ went lest he should see me, till he died.*

Afterwards, when the Muslims fought Musailamah the Liar in the Battle of Yamamah, I went with them. I took with me the same spear that I had killed Hamza with. When the armies met, I saw Musailamah standing with his sword in his hand. I prepared for him, shook my spear till I had full control over it, threw it, and it went into his body. If I killed with this spear the best of people, Hamza, I wish that Allah may forgive me, for I killed with it the worst of people, Musailamah."

Thus, the Lion of Allah and of His Messenger died as a great martyr. His death was as unusual as his life, because it was not enough for his enemies to kill him. They sacrificed all the men and money of the Quraysh to a battle that only sought the Prophet ﷺ and his uncle, Hamza.

Hind bint Utbah, the wife of Abu Sufyan, ordered Wahshi to bring her Hamza's liver, and he responded to her savage desire. When he returned to her, he delivered the liver to her with his right hand, while taking the necklaces with the left as a reward for the accomplished task. Hind, whose father had been killed in the Battle of Badr and whose husband was the leader of the polytheist army, chewed Hamza's liver hoping to relieve her heart, but the liver was too tough for her teeth so she spat it out and stood upon it shouting a poem aloud:

For Badr we've paid you better
In a war more flaring than the other.
I was impatient to avenge the murder of
Utbah, my son, and my brother.
My vow's fulfilled, my heart's relieved forever.

The battle ended and the polytheists mounted their camels and led their horses back to Makkah. The Prophet ﷺ and his Companions examined the battlefield to see the martyrs. There, in the heart of the valley, the Prophet examined the faces of his Companions who had offered their souls to their Lord and had given their lives as a precious sacrifice to Him.

As he did so, the Prophet ﷺ suddenly stood up and looked extremely upset at what he had seen. He ground his teeth and closed his eyes. He never imagined that the Arab moral code could be so savage as to disfigure a dead body in the dreadful way that they had done to his uncle, the Lion of Allah, Hamza ibn Abdul Muttalib. The Prophet ﷺ opened his shining eyes and looked at the dead body of his uncle once more saying, "I will never have a worse loss in my life than yours. I have never been more outraged than I am now."

Then he turned to his Companions saying, "It is only for the sake of Safiyah [Hamza's sister] that she should be grieved and that it should be taken as a practice after me. Otherwise, I would have ordered him to be left without burying so that he may be in the stomachs of beasts and in the claws of birds. If Allah enables me to win over the Quraysh, I will cut thirty of them into pieces."

The Companions shouted in support, "By Allah, if one day we conquer them, we will [attack] them in a way that no Arab has done before!" However, this scene did not end with such desire for revenge. Instead, Allah honoured Hamza by making his death a great lesson for the Muslims to learn justice and mercy, even in situations when retaliation was justified. No sooner had the Prophet finished his threatening words, than a revelation came down to him while he was still standing in his place with the following verse: *Call mankind to the way of your Lord with wisdom and sound advice, and reason with them in a well-mannered way. Indeed, your Lord is well aware of those who have gone astray from His way, and He is well aware of those who are guided. And if you retaliate, let your retaliation be to the extent that you were afflicted, but if you are patient, it will certainly be best for those who are patient; and be patient, yet your patience is only with the help of God, and do not [feel] sorrow for them, not distress yourself at what they devise. Indeed, God is with those who are pious, and those who are doers of good.* (16:125-127)

The revelation of these verses in this situation was the best honour for Hamza. As stated before, the Prophet ﷺ loved him dearly because he was not only an uncle, but also his brother by fosterage, his playmate in childhood and the best friend throughout his life.

The Prophet ﷺ offered the best farewell for Hamza by praying for him repeatedly with the other numerous martyrs that day. Hamza's body was carried to a place of prayer on the battlefield - the same place which had earlier witnessed his bravery and embraced his blood. The Prophet ﷺ and his Companions prayed for Hamza, then they brought another martyr and put him beside Hamza, and prayed for him. Then they would take the martyr away, but leave Hamza and bring the next martyr to place him beside Hamza and pray for him as well. In that way, they brought all the martyrs, one after the other, and prayed for them beside Hamza, who on that day was prayed for a total of 70 times.

---·٠·---

On his way from the battlefield, the Prophet ﷺ heard the women of Banu Abdul Ashhal lamenting their martyrs and he said, "But Hamza has no one to lament him." Sad ibn Muad heard this sentence and thought that the Prophet ﷺ would be satisfied if the women would lament his uncle. He hurried to the women of Banu Abdul Ashhal and ordered them to lament Hamza. When the Prophet heard them doing this he said, "I did not mean this. Go back, may Allah have mercy on you. There will be no crying anymore." The Prophet's ﷺ Companions began to say their eulogies for Hamza in praise of his virtues. The poet Hasan ibn Thabit said in the course of a long poem:

Moan for Hamza, the one
Who won't forget your horse which was old.
He spurs horses, away they run
like lions in jungles. He's strong and bold,
Whiter than Hashim. He looks in the sun
Except for the night, his tongue never told
Among your swords, in was he done,
Paralysed be the hands that Wahshi has sold."

Abdullah ibn Rawahah also said in his poem:
I moaned, but what did moaning do for me?
When they said Hamza the Lion was killed
Abu Yali, a man with honour was filled
For your death, pillars down were pulled.

Safiyah, Hamza's sister and the Prophet's ﷺ aunt, said of Hamza:
To the happy Paradise of Allah he was invited.
Such a destiny for Hamza was what we wanted,
I won't forget you if I stayed or departed.
I moan for a lion by whom Islam was protected.
O brother, may Allah for what you did
Make you rewarded.

But the best words said about him were those of the Prophet ﷺ when he first saw him among the martyrs: "May Allah have mercy on you. You were, as far as I knew, always uniting blood relations and doing all sorts of goodness."

The loss of Hamza was great and nothing could console the Prophet ﷺ for it. But to his surprise, Allah offered him the best consolation.

When he was walking home from Uhud, he saw a woman from the Banu Dinar whose husband, father, and brother had all been killed in the battle. She asked the returning Muslim soldiers about the battle. When they told her of the death of her father, husband, and brother, she soon asked them anxiously, "What about the Prophet of Allah?" They said, "He is very well as you wish him to be." She said, "Show me, let me look at him." They stayed beside her till the Prophet ﷺ came and when she saw him, she said, "If you are safe, all other disasters will be of no importance."

Yes, this was the best condolence for the Prophet ﷺ. He smiled at this unusual situation which had no comparison in loyalty and devotion. A poor, helpless woman lost her father, brother, and husband all in an hour. Her reaction to that news was, "What about the Prophet of Allah?" It was such a well-timed situation that it is evident that Allah planned to console His Prophet ﷺ for the death of Allah's Lion and martyr of all martyrs.

(12)

ABDULLAH IBN MASUD

The First Reciter of Quran

Before the Prophet ﷺ had even established a safe house at Dar Al-Arqam, Ibn Masud had declared his belief in him. He was the sixth one to embrace Islam and follow the Prophet ﷺ. Thus, he was one of the early Muslims.

He narrated his first meeting with the Prophet ﷺ: "I was a young shepherd boy responsible for the sheep of Uqbah ibn Abi Muait. The Prophet once came with Abu Bakr and said, 'O boy, do you have milk for us to drink?' and I said, 'I can't let you drink their milk.' The Prophet ﷺ said, 'Do you have a virgin sheep that has never mated with a male?' I said, 'Yes' and brought it to them. The Prophet ﷺ caught it and stroked its udder and prayed to Allah till the udder filled. Abu Bakr brought him a concave rock into which he milked the sheep. Abu Bakr drank the milk, and then after that the Prophet said to the udder, 'Shrink,' and it did. I went to the Prophet after this incident and said to him, 'Teach me this kind of knowledge.' The Prophet ﷺ said, 'You are already a learned boy'."

Abdullah ibn Masud was fascinated to see the pious Messenger of Allah supplicate, and then milk an udder that should not have been able to produce milk at all. What Ibn Masud did not realise was that he had just witnessed the simplest of Muhammad's miracles, and that he would soon see many more great miracles at the hands of that honourable Prophet; miracles that would fill the world with light and faith. He did not realise either that he himself - the poor, weak, hired shepherd boy working for Uqbah ibn Abi Muait - would be one of those miracles. For he was to become a strong believer, capable of defeating the pride of the Quraysh and overcoming the oppression of its martyrs.

Before his Islam, he never dared to pass by a session attended by any Quraysh nobleman, except with hastened steps and a bowed head. But, after Islam he found himself capable of going to the Kaba, where the elite Quraysh were congregated, standing amongst them and reciting the Quran in a loud, impressive voice: "*In the Name of Allah, the Most Beneficent, the Most Merciful. The Beneficent Allah, taught the Quran. He created man. He taught him eloquent speech. The sun and the moon run on their fixed courses (exactly) calculated with measured out stages for each. And the herbs and the trees both prostrate (to Him)*" (55: 1-6).

He went on reciting while the Quraysh stood thunderstruck, not believing their own eyes or ears. They could not imagine that the one challenging their pride was just one of their hired shepherd boys – poor, unknown Abdullah ibn Masud. Let us hear an eye witness, Az-Zubair (may Allah be pleased with him), describe the scene:

"Abdullah ibn Masud was the first one to recite Quran publicly in Makkah, after the Prophet ﷺ. It happened one day that the Prophet's Companions were gathered with the Prophet ﷺ. They said, 'By Allah, the Quraysh have never heard the Quran being recited to them before. Isn't there any man to recite it so that they may hear it?' Thereupon, Abdullah ibn Masud said, 'I'. They said, 'We are afraid they may harm you. We want a man with a strong family to protect him from those people if they want to harm him.' He said, 'Let me go, Allah will protect me'.

'Ibn Masud went to the Maqam at the Kaba and recited: In the Name of Allah, the Most Beneficent, the Most Merciful. The Beneficent Allah, has taught the Quran... and he went on reciting. The Quraysh gazed at him and said, 'What does Ibn Umm Abd say? He is reciting some of what Muhammad came with.' They went to him and began to beat him in the face while he was reciting, till he finished whatever Allah wished him to recite from the surah. He returned to his friends with a wounded face and body, and they told him, 'This is what we were afraid would happen to you'. He answered them, 'Those enemies of Allah have never been more worthless to me than this moment, and if you wish I will go back to them and do the same tomorrow.' They said, 'No, it is enough for you. You have made them hear what they hated'."

Indeed, when Ibn Masud was fascinated by the sheep's udder which was filled with milk before its time, he did not realise that he and his humble friends would be one of the greater miracles of the Prophet ﷺ on the day they when they would carry the banner of Allah. He did not realise that such a day was very near.

In the meantime, Ibn Masud, was hardly noticeable in the crowd of life, because he was too humble when compared with those who possessed wealth, power, and social status. Financially, he was poor. Physically, he was feeble. And socially, he was non-existent. But Islam compensated him for his poverty with a large share of the treasures of Khosrow and Caesar. Islam also compensated him for his physical weakness with a strong will that conquered the oppressors and helped to change the whole historical course of events. Again, Islam compensated his humble social status through knowledge and honour, that gave him an eminent place in history among the most prominent of historical figures.

The Prophet's prophecy about him which said, "You are a learned boy" was true. Indeed, Allah endowed him with knowledge till he became the most learned of this Ummah and the best one to know Quran by heart. Ibn Masud described himself saying, "I in fact learnt 70 chapters of the Quran directly from the messenger of Allah. I have a better understanding of the Book of Allah than any one of you."

It could be that Allah wanted to reward him for risking his life when he used to recite Quran everywhere during the years of torture. So, He the Almighty endowed him with a wonderful talent for reciting and understanding Quran to the extent that made the Prophet ﷺ direct his Companions to follow his example. The Prophet said, "Stick to the method of Ibn Umm Abd." He recommended that they imitate his way of reciting and learn it from him. The Prophet ﷺ said, "Whoever wants to hear Quran as fresh as it was revealed, let him hear it from Ibn Umm Abd," and said, "Whoever wants to read Quran as fresh as it was revealed, let him read it in the way Ibn Umm Abd does."

It was a pleasure for the Prophet ﷺ to hear the Quran being recited from the mouth of Ibn Masud. The Prophet once called on him and said, "Recite to me, Abdullah," and Abdullah said, "How can I recite to you when it was revealed to you?" The Prophet ﷺ said, "I like to hear it from others," Thereupon Ibn Masud started reading part of Surat An-Nisa till he reached the verse: *How (will it be) then, when We bring from each nation a witness and We bring you as a witness against those people. On that day those who disbelieved and disobeyed the Messenger will wish that they were buried in the earth, but they will never be able to hide a single fact from Allah* (4:41-42). Upon hearing this, the Prophet's eyes flooded with tears and he waved to Ibn Masud saying, "Enough, enough, Ibn Masud."

Ibn Masud often spoke happily about the bounty Allah had bestowed upon him. "By Allah, there is no surah in the Book of Allah about which I do not know where and in what context it was revealed. I have a better understanding of the Book of Allah than you do, and if I were to know that someone had a better understanding than I, and I could reach him on the back of a mule, I would definitely go to him on a camel's back, but I am not better than you are."

The Prophet's Companions confirmed Ibn Masud's knowledge as

well. The Commander of the Faithful, Umar ibn Al-Khattab, said that, "He was filled with knowledge." Abu Musa Al-Ashari also said of Ibn Masud, "Don't ask me about any matter as long as you have this scholar among you." He was not only praised for his knowledge of the Quran and jurisprudence, but also for his piety and God-consciousness. Hudhaifah said about him, "I have never seen anyone more like the Prophet ﷺ in his way of life and characteristics than Ibn Masud." He also said, "The lucky Companions of the Prophet ﷺ realised that Ibn Umm Abd was the nearest one of them to Allah."

One day, a number of Companions were gathered at the house of Ali ibn Abi Talib and said to him, "O Commander of the Faithful, we have never seen a man who is more virtuous, more learned, more companionable, friendly, and God-fearing than Abdullah ibn Masud." Ali said, "I beg you by Allah, is this true from your hearts?" They said, "Yes." Ali replied, "O Allah, I testify in front of You that I say about him like what they said and more. He read the Quran and did what is lawful in it and avoided what is forbidden. He was knowledgeable in religion and scholarly in Sunnah."

The Prophet's Companions also said of him, "He was admitted to the company of the Prophet ﷺ, whereas we were held back, and he was present in his company, whereas we were absent." This means that Ibn Masud often had more privileges than others. He used to enter the Prophet's house and sit with him more than anybody else. He was the one the Prophet ﷺ entrusted with his secrets to the extent that he was nicknamed 'The Secretary'. Abu Musa Al-Ashari (may Allah be pleased with him) said in this context, "I came to Allah's Messenger ﷺ and thought that Ibn Masud was among the members of his family."

The Prophet ﷺ truly admired Ibn Masud for his piety and intelligence. He said about him, "If I were to appoint a commander without consulting the Muslims, I would have appointed Ibn Umm Abd," and as mentioned before, the Prophet ﷺ asked his Companions to "Stick to the method of Ibn Umm Abd."

He was so near to the Prophet ﷺ and so trusted by him that he was given more privileges than anyone else. The Prophet told him, "My permission to you is that you may raise the curtains." This indicates that Ibn Masud was allowed to knock at the Prophet's door at any time during the day or night. This further explains why the Companions said, "He was admitted to the company of the Prophet ﷺ, whereas we were held back..."

Although such a close relationship could have created some sort of relaxed familiarity, Ibn Masud's attitude towards the Prophet ﷺ was always one of respect and politeness. His great esteem for preserving his legacy continued even after the Prophet's death. Although Ibn Masud seldom mentioned the Prophet after his death, in most cases when he did, he began to tremble and shake with anxiety. This occurred whenever his lips began to murmur, "I heard the Prophet ﷺ say ..." lest he should forget or change one single letter of what was said.

Let us hear what his brothers in Islam said about such behaviour. Amr ibn Maimun reported, "I was frequently visited by Ibn Masud for about a year, during which time I did not hear him speak about the Prophet ﷺ. But one day he was talking and he uttered, 'The Prophet ﷺ said...' At this moment he was badly troubled and started to sweat and corrected himself, 'The Prophet ﷺ said something like that'."

Alqamah ibn Qais reported, "Ibn Masud used to speak to people every Thursday night. I never heard him saying, 'The Prophet ﷺ said,' but he once said it and he was leaning on a stick that started to shake in his hand." Also, Masruq narrated on the authority of Abdullah, "One day Ibn Masud was speaking and he said, 'I heard the Prophet ﷺ...' On this he and his clothes started to shake. Then he corrected himself, 'Something like this'." The veneration of the Prophet ﷺ in his heart was so great that he wouldn't dare misremember his words, and this was a sign of his intelligence. Such a man, who accompanied the Prophet more than anybody else, truly knew how magnanimous the Prophet ﷺ was. Therefore, he maintained the same level of veneration for him, both during his life and after his death.

Ibn Masud never missed the company of the Prophet ﷺ either while travelling or at home. He participated in all the battles, and on the Day of Badr his role was significant, especially with Abu Jahl. The Prophet's Caliphs, were also fully aware of his proper value. The Commander of the Faithful, Umar ibn Al-Khattab, appointed him as director of the treasury in Kufa and he said to the people there, "By Allah, there is no god but He. You know that I have given you a preference over myself when I sent him to you to learn from [Ibn Masud]."

The people of Kufa liked him as they never liked anyone before him. It was a real miracle, as the people of Kufa were renowned for their inability to tolerate peace, and rarely agreed on liking one kind of food, let alone a leader. Their love for him was so great that when the Caliph Uthman (may Allah be pleased with him) wanted to discharge him of his office, they surrounded him and said, "Stay with us and don't go. We will protect you against anything that you don't like." But Ibn Masud gave them an answer that really reflected his greatness and piety. He said, "He has the right of obedience from me. There will be turbulence coming and I hate to be the first to open the door to it."

This wonderful situation discloses to us the nature of the relationship between Ibn Masud and Uthman. They had an argument and a disagreement between them which ended with the Caliph cutting Ibn Masud's salary from the Bait Al-Mal. But in return, Ibn Masud never spoke ill of the Caliph. On the contrary, he used to defend him. When he heard about the attempted assassinations on Uthman, he said famously, "If they kill him, they will not find anyone like him to succeed." Some of Ibn Masud's friends said, "We never heard him uttering a bad word about Uthman."

Allah endowed Ibn Masud with wisdom along with his piety. He had an insight that enabled him to see facts beyond the surface, and the capability to express such facts in an intelligent manner. For example, he summarised the life of Umar ibn Al-Khattab in one concise sentence: "Umar's Islam was an opening, his hijra was a victory, and his rule was a mercy."

Once, he even expressed the idea of the relativity of time by saying, "Your Lord does not have day or night, because the light of the earth and the skies is but from the light of His face." In another context he praised the value of work in raising the social standard of man: "I hate a man living in leisure with nothing to do, either for his worldly life or the life to come." And, finally, he said more comprehensively: "The best wealth is the wealth of the soul. The best provision is right conduct. The most major of sins is lying, the most evil earning is usury, and the most evil of what can be consumed is the consumption of the orphan's property. Whoever excuses others, will be excused by Allah, and whoever forgives others will be forgiven by others."

That was Abdullah ibn Masud, the Prophet's ﷺ Companion, and that is but one glimpse of the heroic life he lived in the way of Allah, His Prophet and His religion. That was the man who had been as small as a bird. He was so lightweight and short that he was the same height of a sitting person. He had very thin legs. He once climbed a tree to pick some arak sticks for the Prophet ﷺ, and when the Companions saw how thin his legs were they laughed. The Prophet said, "Are you laughing at Ibn Masud's legs? On Allah's scales of justice, they are heavier than the mountain of Uhud." Indeed, that was the poor and weak boy who became by faith a leader, guiding people to the light.

It was Allah's bounty on him that he was counted among the first ten Companions of the Prophet ﷺ who were promised to enter Paradise while they were still alive. He participated in all the victorious wars with the Prophet and his Caliphs. He witnessed how the two greatest empires of the time opened their gates in submission to the banner of Islam. He saw high positions and lucrative money pouring into the hands of the Muslims, but his mind was never occupied by such matters. Instead, he was concerned only with how to fulfil his pledge to the Prophet ﷺ, and he was also never tempted to give up the life of humbleness and self-denial that he used to lead. In fact, he had only one wish that he dreamed all his life might come true. Let us hear him speak about it:

"While I was with the Prophet ﷺ at the Battle of Tabuk, I woke up at midnight to see a flame of fire near the place of the army. I followed it and found the Prophet ﷺ, Abu Bakr and Umar digging a grave to bury Abdullah Dhul Bijadain Al-Muzani who died at the time. The Prophet ﷺ was in the grave and asked Abu Bakr and Umar, 'Hand your brother to me', and they did. After he put his body in the grave he said, 'O Allah, in this night I am fully satisfied and pleased with him. So I beg You to be satisfied with him.' Upon hearing this Ibn Mas'ud said, "I wish I were him (he meant Dhul-Bijadain)."

This was his sole wish in life, to be admired completely and prayed for by the Prophet himself ﷺ. It was not related to what people race towards in this world, such as wealth, social status or glory. It was the wish of a man who possessed a kind heart, a noble soul, and a strong faith. Such a man was guided by Allah, educated by the Prophet ﷺ, and enlightened by the Quran.

(13)

HUDHAIFAH IBN AL-YAMMAN

The Enemy of Hypocrisy, the Friend of Frankness

The people of Mada'in came out in great numbers to welcome their new governor chosen by their Caliph Umar (may Allah be pleased with him). They came out with great enthusiasm in the graceful Companion, who they had heard much about. News of his good conduct, his piety, and his great achievement in the conquest of Iraq all preceded his arrival.

While they were waiting for the coming procession, they saw before them a bright fellow riding on a donkey with an old saddle. The man was riding with his legs hanging, holding a loaf of bread and some salt in his hands, and chewing on his food. When he came in their midst, they discovered that he was in fact Hudhaifah ibn Al-Yamman! But why the surprise? Who did they expect Umar's choice would be? Truly though, they were not to blame. Their countries had not been accustomed to having rulers with such simple grace, since before the time of the Persians.

And so, Hudhaifah was surrounded and welcomed by many people. When he saw that they were gazing at him as if expecting a speech, he looked at them closely and said, "Beware of sedition!" They asked, "What is sedition, Abu Abdullah?" "The gates of rulers," he said. "When one of you is admitted to the presence of the ruler or governor and falsely agrees with what he says and commends him for what he has not done." It was a wonderful start, as much as it was surprising. People at once remembered what they had heard about their new governor — that he did not detest anything in the whole world as much as he detested hypocrisy. Such a beginning was the truest expression of the new governor's character. It was to be indicative of his style of government and rule.

As a matter of fact, Hudhaifah ibn Al-Yamman was a man who detested hypocrisy so much that he had the remarkable capability to detect it even in the most concealed of places. He and his brother Safwan once came to the Prophet ﷺ, accompanied by their father, and they all embraced Islam. He added more sharpness and polish to his inborn qualities from that day forward; when he embraced a powerful and modest religion that scorned cowardice, hypocrisy, and lies.

Moreover, he learned his manners at the hands of the Messenger ﷺ who was as clear as the morning light. Nothing was hidden in his life, nor in his inner self. He was truthful and trustworthy. He too liked those who were strong in their righteousness, and detested those who were not straightforward. Therefore, there was no place where his talent could bloom more than it did under the Messenger's guidance and among that generation of his great Companions.

Verily, his talent grew and developed. Hudhaifah found his speciality in reading faces and probing into the inner self. At a glance he could easily know the secrets of a person's hidden depths. He was so impressive that the intelligent and resourceful Caliph Umar often asked for Hudhaifah's opinion and insight in selecting and knowing men.

Hudhaifah recognised that what is good in this world is obvious to whoever seeks it, and that evil is very often disguised and hidden. Therefore, the intelligent person should be discrete in studying evil in its hidden and apparent forms. He therefore devoted his time to the study of evil and evil doers, as well as hypocrisy and hypocrites. He reported:

"People used to ask Allah's Prophet ﷺ about good, but I used to ask him about evil, for fear that it should overtake me. I said, 'O Messenger of Allah, we were in ignorant and evil times, then Allah presented us with this good. Will there be evil after this good?' He said, 'Yes.' I said, 'And after this evil, will there be good?' He said, 'Yes but it would be tainted with evil (literally, smoke).' I asked, 'What will this evil be?' He said, 'There will be some people who will lead (people) according to principles other than my tradition. You will see their actions and disapprove of them.' I said, 'Will there be any evil after that good?' He said, 'Yes, there will be some people who will invite others to the doors of Hell, and whoever accepts their invitation to it will be thrown in it (by them)'.

'I said, 'O Messenger of Allah! Describe those people to us.' He said, 'They will belong to us and speak our language.' I asked, 'What do you order me to do if such a thing should take place in my life?' He said, 'Adhere to the group of Muslims and their chief.' I asked, 'If there is neither a group (of Muslims), nor a chief, what shall I do?' He said, 'Keep away from all those different sects, even if you have to eat the roots of a tree, till you meet Allah while you are still in that state'."

Note Hudhaifah's statement, "People used to ask Allah's Prophet ﷺ about good, but I used to ask him about evil, for fear that it should overtake me." Hudhaifah ibn Al-Yamman lived his life with eyes open and paid particular attention to temptations and the paths to evil, so that he might avoid them and warn people of them. This gave him insight into the world, experience with people, and knowledge of the times. He would contemplate matters in his mind as a philosopher would and with the sound judgment of a wise man. He said (may Allah be pleased with him):

"Almighty Allah sent Muhammad ﷺ to call people from misguidance to the right path, and from disbelief to belief in Allah. Some responded to his call, following the right way. Those who were dead were raised to life and those who were alive died because of their evil doing. When the period of prophethood was over, caliphates followed the same methods. Then there appeared a detested monarchy. There were people who disavowed with their hearts, hands, and tongues, and who responded to the path of justice. There were those who disavowed with their hearts and tongues but abstained from using their hands. Thus, they left out an area of justice. There were also those who disavowed with their hearts, abstaining to use their hands or tongues. Thus, they left out two areas of justice. There were those who did not disavow, neither with their hearts, nor with their hands or tongues, and those were the living dead!

He talked about hearts, and a life of guidance or misguidance, according to the heart. He said: "There are four kinds of hearts: a locked heart, which is the heart of the disbeliever; a deceitful heart, which is the heart of the hypocrite; a pure heart full of light, which is the heart of the believer; and a heart filled with hypocrisy and faith. Its faith is like a tree supplied with good water, but like hypocrisy because it is like an ulcer filled with pus and blood. Whichever is made will win."

Hudhaifah's experience of evil, and his persistence in resisting it, sharpened his tongue and words. He himself informed us about this in a noble hadith: "I approached the Prophet ﷺ and said, 'O Messenger of Allah, I have an abusing tongue towards my people, and I am afraid it might lead me to the fire of Hell.' The Prophet ﷺ said to me, 'Do you ask Allah's forgiveness? I repent to Allah a hundred times a day.'"

That was Hudhaifah, the enemy of hypocrisy and the friend of honesty. For a man of this character, his faith had to be strong and his loyalty intense. He even witnessed his father die in the battle of Uhud, killed in error by Muslim hands, when they mistook him for one of the unbelievers. Hudhaifah was looking around when by chance he saw the swords attacking his father. He called to them, "My father! My father! He's my father!" But it was too late. When the Muslims heard about this incident they were sincerely grieved, but Hudhaifah looked at them with mercy and forgiveness and said, "May Allah forgive you. He is the Most Merciful." He then went forward with his sword towards the raging battle, doing his best and performing his duty.

When the battle ended and the Prophet ﷺ heard the news, he ordered that blood money be paid for the death of Hudhaifah's father, Husail ibn Jabur (may Allah be pleased with him). However, Hudhaifah refused to take the money and gave it as alms to the Muslims, an act which made the Prophet love and appreciate him even more.

Hudhaifah's faith and loyalty refused to acknowledge inability and weakness, or even the impossible. In the Battle of Khandaq (after the failure of the unbelievers of the Quraysh and their Jewish allies), the Prophet ﷺ wanted to know the latest developments in the enemy camp. The night was black and terrifying, and a storm was raging as if it would uproot the mountains. The whole situation, which included a stubborn siege, brought about extreme hunger, fear and anxiety. Therefore, who would have the strength to go amidst the dark dangers of the enemy camp, and penetrate it to gather intelligence? The Messenger ﷺ was the one who selected this person from among his Companions to perform such a difficult task. Who was that hero? It was Hudhaifah ibn Al-Yamman. The Prophet asked him and he obeyed.

He admitted with great candour that he had no choice but to obey, thus implying that he feared the mission being assigned to him. He was afraid of its consequences. His fear was due to performing this mission under the pinch of hunger, cold weather, and extreme exhaustion – all from the siege of the disbelievers that had lasted a month or more.

But still, he pressed on. He covered the distance between the two armies and penetrated the surrounding enemy camp of the Quraysh. A violent wind had put out the camp's fires, so the place was enveloped in darkness. Hudhaifah took his place amidst the lines of the fighters. The leader of the Quraysh, Abu Sufyan, was afraid that darkness might surprise them with scouts from the Muslim camp. He stood to warn his army, and Hudhaifah heard his loud voice saying, "O people of the Quraysh, each one of you should know who is sitting next to him and should know his name." Hudhaifah reports, "I hastened to the hand of the man next to me, and said to him, 'Who are you?' He said, 'Such and such a person!'

He therefore secured his being with the army in peace! Abu Sufyan resumed his talk to the army, saying, "O people of the Quraysh, by Allah, you are not in a place to settle. The horses and the camels are exhausted. The tribe of Banu Quraidah has betrayed us and we learned about them what we hate, and we suffer from the violent wind as you see. No food can be cooked, no fire can blaze for us, and no structure can hold. You have to leave, for I am leaving." He then mounted his camel and started moving, followed by the fighters.

Hudhaifah said, "But for the promise I gave Allah's Messenger ﷺ, who asked me not to do anything until I returned to him, I would have killed him with an arrow." Hudhaifah then returned to the Messenger and gave him the information and happy news.

---•◊•---

Whoever saw Hudhaifah and considered his way of thinking, his philosophy, and his devotion to knowledge could hardly expect any heroism from him in the battlefield. Nevertheless, Hudhaifah contradicted all expectations.

The contemplative man, who used to worship Allah in solitude, changed in an instant on carrying his sword. Suffice to say that he was one of only three or five who had the great privilege of invading all the cities of Iraq. In Hamdan, and Ar-Raiy Ad-Dainawar, the conquest was accomplished through him. In the great Battle of Nahawand, in which the Persians gathered about 150,000 fighters, Caliph Umar chose An-Numan ibn Muqrin to lead the Muslim armies, then wrote to Hudhaifah to march to him leading an army from Kufa.

Umar sent his letter to the fighters, saying, "When the Muslims gather, let every commander lead his army, and let An- Numan ibn Muqrin be the commander-in-chief of all the armies. If An-Numan is martyred, let Hudhaifah be the leader. If he is martyred, let Jarir ibn Abdullah lead them." In this way, the Commander of the Faithful went on choosing the leaders of the battle till he named seven of them. Then the two armies met.

The Persians were 150,000, while the Muslims were only 30,000. A battle, which exceeded all others, commenced. It was one of the fiercest in history, in terms of violence and heroism. The leader of the Muslim army, An-Numan ibn Muqrin fell in battle and was martyred, but before the Muslim standard fell to the ground, the new leader caught it with his right hand, and led the wind of victory with vigour and great heroism. This leader was none other but Hudhaifah ibn Al-Yamman.

He quickly held the standard and decided not to announce the news of the death of An-Numan until the battle was over. He called Naim ibn Muqrin to be in the place of his brother to honour him. How he achieved all this in no time, in the heart of the battle, was solely through his bright intuition. Then, he turned the head of his horse towards the fighters of his army and called, "O you followers of Muhammad ﷺ, here are Allah's Gardens ready to receive you, do not let them wait long. Come on, men of the Battle of Badr! Proceed, O you heroes of the Battle of Khandaq, Uhud, and Tabuk!" Hudhaifah fired up the enthusiasm of the soldiers and the battle concluded in an overwhelming defeat for the Persians.

Hudhaifah always exercised his wisdom, whether on the battlefield or at home when advice was asked of him. For instance, when Sa'ad ibn Abu Waqqas and the Muslims with him needed to escape persecution in Mada'in, Umar wrote to Sa'ad once a safe space had been found for resettlement. Who was deputed to choose the site and the place? It was Hudhaifah, accompanied by Salman ibn Ziyad. When they reached the land of Kufa, it was a barren, sandy land, full of pebbles, but Hudhaifah sensed only an atmosphere of healing and good health. He said to his companion, "This [is the] place, Allah willing." That was how Kufa was planned, and the hands of construction turned it into an inhabited city. As soon as the Muslims migrated there, the sick were cured, the weak became strong, and their veins pulsed with good health.

Hudhaifah was very intelligent and had various experiences. He always used to say to the Muslims, "Your best are not those who neglect this world for the last, nor those who neglect the last for this world. The best are those who take from this and that."

In the year 36 AH, Hudhaifah was finally called to meet his Lord. While he was getting ready for his very last journey, some of his companions came to see him. He asked them, "Have you brought a shroud with you?" They said, "Yes." He said, "Show it to me." When he saw it, he found it was new and too long. One last sarcastic grin was drawn on his lips, and he said, "This is not a shroud for me. Two white wraps without a shirt are sufficient for me. I will not be left in the grave for a long time, but will be offered a better place or a worse one!"

He then murmured a few words which, when they listened to them, they discerned the following: "Welcome, O death! A dear thing coming after longing. The one who repents now, prospers not." And with that, one of the most humble, pious and illuminating human souls was raised to Allah.

(14)

AMMAR IBN YASIR

A Man of Paradise

If there were ever people born in Paradise, brought to maturity there, and then sent down to earth merely to adorn it, then Ammar, his mother Sumayya and his father Yasir would certainly be play a part! Of course, Yasir's family were in fact people of Paradise. As Allah's Messenger ﷺ once reassured them, "Patience, O Yasir's family. Verily, your meeting place will be in Paradise." So, let us learn more about this blessed family.

---·◊·---

Ammar's father, Yasir ibn Amir, left his native place in Yemen seeking a brother of his. In Makkah he found an appealing place, so he settled there and formed an alliance with Abu Hudhaifah ibn Al-Mughirah, who married Yasir to one of his slave women, Sumayya bint Khayyat. Allah granted the blessed parents a son, Ammar. They embraced Islam early, and like those other righteous early Muslims, they had their good share of the Quraysh's persecution and terror.

The Quraysh used to waylay the believers to attack them. If the believers were among the honourable and noble people in their community, the Quraysh would pursue them with threats and menace. Abu Jahl would meet one of the believers and tell him, "You abandoned your forefathers' religion and they were better than you. We will spoil your character, degrade your honour, reduce your trade, and exhaust your money." They would then launch a heated war of nerves upon him.

If the believers were among the weak, poor, or slaves of Makkah, then the Quraysh would burn them with the fire of persecution. Yasir's family belonged to that class. The order for their persecution was handed to Banu Makhzum. They used to take them all - Yasir, Sumayya and Ammar - to the burning desert of Makkah, where they would pour upon them different kinds of the hell. Sumayya's share of that torment was terrible. We shall not go into detail about her torture here, but suffice to say the martyred Sumayya maintained such a firm stance that day that she was known thereafter as a truly great mother to believers from all ages, and indeed to all honourable people throughout the ages.

---·◊·---

The Messenger ﷺ used to go where he knew Yasir's family were being tortured to see them. At that time though, he had no means of resistance or keeping them from harm. This was Allah's will, because the new faith revealed to Muhammad - the faith of 'Ibrahim Al-Hanifan' (Abraham the true) - was not just a passing reform. It was a whole new way of life for humanity, a religion to be inherited along with its history of heroism, sacrifices, and risks. These abundant noble sacrifices are the foundations that grant an everlasting firmness to the faith. It is the beacon that guides the coming generations to the reality of this religion, to its truth and greatness.

Therefore, Islam had to make its sacrifices, the meaning of which is illustrated in more than one verse of the Quran. Allah says:

Do the people think that they will be left to say: "We believe", and they shall not be tried? (29:2).

Do You think that you will enter Paradise before Allah tests those of you who fought (in His Cause) and (also) tests those who remained patient? (3:142).

And we indeed tested those who were before them. And Allah will certainly make (it) known (the truth of) those who are true, and will certainly make (it) known (the falsehood of) those who are liars, (although Allah Knows all that before putting them to test). (29:3)

Do you think you shall be left alone while Allah has not yet tested those among you who have striven hard... (9:16)

Allah will not leave the believers in the state in which you are now, until He distinguishes the wicked from the good. (3:179)

And what you suffered (of the disaster) on the day (of the Battle of Uhud when) the two armies met, was by the leave of Allah, in order that He might test the believers. (3:166)

This is how the Quran taught both its bearers and its inheritors the key virtues of Islam. Namely, that sacrifice is the essence of faith, and that resistance of injustice is achieved through firm perseverance and patience. When Islam was laying down its foundations and establishing its principles, it required purification through sacrifice. In carrying out this great mission, a number of its disciples were chosen as role models and elevated as examples for the believers still to come. Sumayya, Yasir and Ammar were a part of this blessed group.

We said that Allah's Messenger ﷺ used to go out every day to Yasir's family, to commend their fortitude and heroism. His heart melted out of mercy to see them so severely tortured. One day while he was looking for them, Ammar called to him, "O Messenger of Allah, we are suffering from extreme torment." The Messenger called to him saying, "Patience, Abu Yaqdhan, patience O Yasir's family. Verily, your meeting place will be in Paradise."

Ammar's companions described the torture that was inflicted upon him in many of their reports. Amr ibn Al-Hakam, for instance, said, "Ammar used to be tortured so much that he would not be aware of what he was saying." Amr ibn Maimun said, "The polytheists scorched Ammar ibn Yasir with fire, and Allah's Messenger ﷺ used to pass by him, pass his hand over Yasir's head and say, 'O fire, be cool and peaceful on Ammar, as you were cool and peaceful on Ibrahim.'"

Despite that overwhelming terror, it did not vanquish Ammar's spirit. Ammar did not feel utterly ruined except on one day - when his executioners employed all their skill in crime and injustice. They burned his skin with fire, laid him on the heated sands of the desert under burning stones, then submerged him in water until he could hardly breathe and his wounds were laid bare to the skin. On that day, when he fell unconscious under the effect of that horror, they said to him, "Say something good about our gods." They kept saying things which he repeated without being conscious of what he was saying.

When he became aware, he recalled what he had said and this made him extremely upset. He saw this mistake as an unforgivable sin, and his guilt for it made him suffer so much that when the torture resumed, it seemed like a balm to his troubled soul. He was enduring the dreadful anguish of the body because his spirit was strong before, but now he felt defeated and became overburdened with the fear of death. It was then Almighty Allah who sent an angel with its right hand outstretched to Ammar. Shaking his hand, the angel called to him saying, "Get up, O hero! There is no blame or embarrassment for you."

When Allah's Messenger ﷺ met him, he found him crying. Wiping Ammar's tears away, the Prophet asked him, "The polytheists took you, ducked your head in water, and you said such and such a thing?" Ammar answered him, still crying, "Yes, O Messenger of Allah." Allah's Messenger ﷺ smiled and said, "If they repeat it, say the same thing." Then he recited the glorious Quranic verse: *...except him who is forced* *thereto and whose heart is at rest with faith...* (16:106)

Ammar's tranquillity was restored, he no longer felt pain when they punished him, and he no longer cared about it. His spirit and his faith conquered. Ammar remained steadfast until his tormentors were exhausted and they finally retreated, yielding to his determination.

The Muslims settled in Medina after the hijra of their Messenger. The Islamic community there began to take shape very fast. Within that group of believers, Ammar was allocated a dignified position. Allah's Messenger loved him greatly and used to boast among his Companions about Ammar's faith and guidance. He said about him, "Verily, Ammar is filled to the bones with faith."

When a slight misunderstanding took place between Khalid ibn Al-Walid and Ammar, the Messenger said, "Whoever antagonises Ammar is antagonised by Allah, and whoever detests Ammar is detested by Allah." Thereupon, Khalid ibn Al-Walid, Islam's very own hero, hastened to Ammar, apologised to him and begged his forgiveness.

When the Messenger and his Companions were building the mosque in Medina, Imam Ali composed a song and kept on repeating it with other Muslims, saying:

He who frequents the mosques,
Remaining there standing and sitting,
Is not equal to the one who keeps away from dust.

Ammar was working at the side of the mosque, so he kept repeating the song, with a raised voice. One of his companions thought that Ammar was in fact disparaging him. He therefore spoke angrily to Ammar, which angered the Messenger of Allah, and he said, "What is their business with Ammar? He calls them to Heaven and they call him to Hell. To me, Ammar is but a skin between my eyes and my nose."

When the Messenger of Allah loves a man that much, this man's faith, his accomplishment, his loyalty, his conscience, and manners must have reached the pinnacle of human achievement. That was Ammar. Allah had granted him abundant blessings and guidance. The Messenger commended his piety and offered him as a role model when he said, "Take the examples of the two succeeding me, Abu Bakr and Umar, and follow the guidance of Ammar." The narrators described him, saying, "He was tall, with blueish-black eyes, broad-shouldered, among the most silent of the people and the least talkative."

So, what became of Ammar's life, after he endured the scars of torture and he went on to become a loyal disciple? Well, alongside his guide, the Messenger ﷺ, he partook in all the key battles of early Islam: Badr, Uhud, Khandaq, Tabuk and others. When the Messenger of Allah ﷺ passed away, the outstanding Companion marched on. When the Muslims faced the Persians and then the Romans, Ammar was always there in the first line, an honest and brave soldier who did not miss an opportunity to defend his faith.

As well as brave, he was also a pious and humble believer. As such, when Caliph Umar ibn Al-Khattab was carefully choosing governors for the Muslims, his trust lay inherently with Ammar ibn Yasir. After making him the governor of Kufa, he wrote to the people there heralding their new appointment and said, "I send you Ammar ibn Yasir as a governor, and Ibn Masud as a teacher and a minister. They are of the distinguished people of Muhammad's Companions, and of the people of Badr."

During his rule, Ammar pursued a way which was hard for the more materialistic people to follow, so much so that they even considered rebelling. Regardless, his rule had made him more modest, more pious, and even more ascetic. One of his contemporaries in Kufa, Ibn Abu Hudhail said about him, "I saw Ammar ibn Yasir when he was the governor of Kufa buying some vegetables. He tied them with a rope and carried them on his shoulders and went home."

When he was governor, a member of the public tried to scorn him by calling to him with the phrase, "O you, whose ear is cut off." This ear had been cut off by the apostate swords during the Yamamah War. Abdullah ibn Umar (may Allah be pleased with him) reported about Ammar's injury: "I saw Ammar ibn Yasir on the Day of Yamamah on a rock shouting, "O you Muslim people, are you running away from Paradise? I am Ammar ibn Yasir, come to me." When I looked at him, I found his ear cut off and swinging while he was fighting fiercely." How did Ammar respond to this insult in Kufa then? Despite having the advantage of power on his side, he did not rise to the insult, but merely said, "You insulted the best part of my ear. It was injured in the cause of Allah."

There are many such examples of good character among the Prophet's Companions. If anyone has his doubts concerning Muhammad ﷺ, he should ask himself, "Would anyone but a noble messenger and great teacher be able to inspire this kind of behaviour in others?" If his Companions were asked to fight for Allah's cause, they hastened to it. His Caliphs, Abu Bakr and Umar, were nothing but humble and would personally milk the orphans' sheep and bake their bread for them. Muhammad's ﷺ governors carried their food on their backs, tied with a rope, as Ammar did; or gave up their pay and set to making baskets and vessels out of plaited palm leaves, as Salman did. Should we not bow in salutation and respect to the faith that produced them and to the Messenger who raised them? And before all, to Almighty Allah Who chose them for that, and made them pioneers to the best nation on earth?

Hudhaifah ibn Al-Yamman, who was an expert in perceptiveness, was in his death throes when his companions around him asked, "To whom should we go, if people differ?" Hudhaifah answered in his last words, "You should turn to Ibn Sumayya, because he will not part from truth until death." Now, let us trace Ammar's truthful path and follow the landmark events in his great life.

After the Muslims had settled in Medina, the Messenger ﷺ and his righteous Companions, set about establishing and building Allah's mosque. Their faithful hearts were filled with joy as they worked with hope - carrying stone, mixing mortar, and erecting the building. There was a team here, a team there – all singing with overjoyed voices, "O Allah, living is but in the next world, then have mercy on the Ansar and the Muhajirun!"

They all worked hard, by carrying Allah's banner and erecting His building. The kind Messenger ﷺ was with them, carrying the heaviest of the stones and performing the hardest of work alongside them. Ammar ibn Yasir was there amidst the celebration, carrying the heavy stones from their quarries, into position. When Muhammad the Messenger of Allah saw him, he sympathised greatly with him. He walked over to him, and removed the dust from his head with his hand. He contemplated Ammar's innocent, faithful face and said in front of all the Companions. "Alas for Ibn Sumayya, killed by the tyrant group."

Soon after, a wall that Ammar was working beneath collapsed, and some mistakenly thought Ammar to be dead. They went to offer condolences to the Messenger ﷺ, and the Companions were shocked by the news, but the Messenger reassuringly said, "Ammar is not dead. The tyrant party will kill Ammar." Who was this party? Where and when? Ammar listened to the prophecy in a way that showed he knew the truth of Muhammad's perception. Yet, he was not horrified, as since becoming a Muslim, he had been expecting death and martyrdom every day.

―――――・◊・―――――

Days and years passed. The Messenger ﷺ returned to Allah, the Supreme Companion, followed by Abu Bakr and then Umar (may Allah be pleased with them all). Uthman ibn Affan, 'The Man of Two Lights', had now become Caliph. Conspiracies against Islam were doing their best, trying to gain by treachery and sedition what they lost in war. Umar's assassination was the first success achieved by these conspiracies. A breeze of ill will blew over Medina. Roused on by Umar's martyrdom, those countries whose thrones Islam had unseated, were soon rebelling once more. Arguably, Uthman might not have given the matter the response it deserved, and so his own martyrdom sadly followed thereafter.

Now, Muawiyah had begun fighting the new Caliph, Ali, contesting his right to the caliphate. The Companions had different stances. Some of them washed their hands of the whole matter, making Ibn Umar's words their motto:

> *To the one who says, "Come to prayer," I will respond.*
> *To the one who says, "Come to success," I will respond.*
> *But to the one who says, "Come to kill your Muslim brother,*
> *And to take his money," I will say, "No."*

Some Muslims were partial to Ali, who commanded the pledge of allegiance to him as Caliph, whilst others preferred Muawiyah. But, where did Ammar stand on this? His opinion was valued, as this was the man about whom the Prophet said: "Follow the guidance of Ammar," and, "Whoever antagonises Ammar, will be antagonised by Allah". The man who, if he approached the house of Allah's Messenger ﷺ, the Prophet would say, "Welcome the good-scented, kind man, allow him to come in".

In fact, Ammar stood by Ali ibn Abi Talib, not out of bias or prejudice, but to stand on the side of truth. Ali was the Caliph of the Muslims and had the pledge of allegiance to be its leader. He took the caliphate and he was worthy of it. Above all, Ali was to the Messenger as was Harun (Aron) to Musa (Moses). Ammar, who always turned towards the truth wherever he found it, turned to Ali and stood by him.

Ali (may Allah be pleased with him) was overjoyed with Ammar's pledge and trusted that he was in the right because the truthful Ammar ibn Yasir went with him. The terrible Day of Siffin arrived. Imam Ali came out to face the now serious rebellion, which he felt he had to curb. Ammar came out with him, even though he was 93 years old by then. It is hard to imagine a man of 93 readying for battle, but he fought as strongly as a man of 30.

Ammar was a man who was often silent. He would usually only move his lips to supplicate, "I seek Allah's protection from sedition. I seek Allah's protection from sedition." And after the passing of the Messenger of Allah ﷺ, these words remained his constant supplication. As the days passed, he sought Allah's protection even more, as if his pure heart felt the impending danger. When the sedition finally occurred, Ibn Sumayya knew his place. And so, at the age of 93, he stood at Siffin with sword in hand to support a cause he thought worthy.

He said of that fight: "O people, let us be directed to the people who claim they are avenging Uthman. By Allah, their intention is not revenge, but they have tasted worldly things and are pleased with them. They know that truth keeps them away from what they enjoy of lust and their world. Those people had no precedent in the past to keep Muslims in obedience to them or in their support. Their hearts have not felt awe towards Allah to force them to follow the truth. They deceive the people by claiming they are avenging Uthman's death. They seek nothing but to be tyrants and kings."

Then, he took the standard in his hand, raised it high and as it fluttered above their heads he shouted, "By Allah in Whose hands my soul lies, I fought with this standard with the Messenger of Allah, and here I am fighting with it today. By Allah, if they defeat us until they reach the palm trees of Hajar, I would still believe we are in the right and they are following the wrong." People followed Ammar and trusted in his wisdom. Abu Abdur Rahman As-Sulami reported: "We witnessed with Ali the Battle of Siffin, and I saw Ammar not taking one turn nor one of its valleys but the Companions of Muhammad ﷺ would follow him as if he were their standard!"

When Ammar was engaged in the battle he knew that he would be one of its martyrs. The Messenger's prophecy sat firmly in his thoughts: "The tyrant party will kill Ammar." For that reason, his voice was ringing over the horizon with the following tune, "Today, I meet the dear ones, Muhammad and his Companions." He would then rush like a high arrow towards Muawiyah's position and surround him, singing loudly:

We hit you at its first revelation,
Now we hit you again for its interpretation;
A hitting that removes respect from one's eyes,
And distracts the lover from his lass,
Or restores the right to its own place.

He meant by this that the former Companions of the Messenger ﷺ (of whom Ammar was one) had fought the Quraysh's Umayyads in the past. They had fought them after the Quran openly commanded them to fight the disbelievers. But at Siffin, even though they were facing Muslims and were not openly commanded by the Quran to fight them, Ammar's understanding of the Holy Book persuaded him to fight. They hoped that the usurped right would be restored to its people, and the fire of rebellion would be extinguished once and for all. It also signified that in the past they fought the Umayyads for their disbelief in faith and in the Quran. Today they were fighting them for deviating from faith and for turning away from the Quran. They fought them for their incorrect interpretations, and their attempts to alter Quranic verses for their own ends.

This man of 93 was involved in the last battle of his noble and brave life. Through this act, he gave us a final lesson in perseverance for the truth. Most of Muawiyah's men actually avoided Ammar so as not to kill him and be labelled the 'tyrant party' Muhammad ﷺ spoke of. Yet,

Ammar fought as if he were a whole army in himself, and his bravery enraged some of the soldiers.

Muawiyah's army had many soldiers from the newer group of Muslims - those who embraced the faith after the Islamic conquest had liberated them from Roman and Persian rule. Most of these soldiers fuelled the civil war by encouraging Muawiyah's refusal to pledge allegiance to Ali as Caliph. The disagreement, although serious, could have ended peacefully if the affairs had remained with the early Muslims. However, no sooner it was formed, it was seized by hands that did not care for the fate of Islam. Instead of calming matters, they kept adding fuel to the discord. At noon, the news of Ammar's death spread, and the Muslims went on repeating to one another the prophecy of Allah's Messenger ﷺ which had been heard by all the Companions on the day of the festival while building the mosque: "Alas for Ibn Sumayya, killed by the tyrant party."

Now it was clear who the 'tyrant party' was. It was the one that had killed Ammar, none other than Muawiyah's army. Ali's Companions became more and more convinced of this fact. As for Muawiyah's party though, their hearts became suspicious, and some prepared to switch side to Ali. No sooner did Muawiyah hear of what had happened than he came out announcing to the people that the prophecy was right, and the Messenger ﷺ really prophesied that Ammar was going to be killed by the tyrant party. But who killed Ammar? Then he shouted to the people of his party, "He was surely killed by those who brought this old man out of his house and accompanied him to the battlefield." Some people who were inclined towards that interpretation were deceived, and the battle continued.

As for Ammar, Imam Ali carried him on his chest to where he and the other Muslims prayed, and there he was buried. Muslims stood at his grave wondering whether Ammar knew what fate awaited him that day. Only a few hours before, Ammar had been singing at the battlefield, filled with the delight of a tired stranger who was returning happily home. He had been shouting, "Today I meet the dear ones, Muhammad and his Companions." Did he have a meeting time set with them?

Some Companions approached each other, and one asked, "Do you remember the twilight of that day in Medina when we were sitting with Allah's Messenger ﷺ and suddenly his face brightened and he said, 'Paradise is longing for Ammar'?" His friend answered, "Yes, on that day he mentioned others, among which were Ali, Salman and Bilal."

Paradise was indeed longing for Ammar. The longing remained whilst he accomplished his worldly tasks and achievements. Was it not then time to comply with the call from Paradise? Surely, it was; and good is rewarded only with good. When the dust of his grave was being levelled on his body by his companions, Ammar's soul was already embracing its happy destiny - there in the eternity of Paradise.

(15)

UBADAH IBN AS- SAMIT

A Representative in Allah's Party

The Prophet ﷺ once said, "If the Ansar chose to move in a certain direction, I would follow them. By Allah, if there had been no emigration, I would have chosen to be one of the Ansar." Ubadah ibn As-Samit was not only one of the Ansar spoken of, but also one of their renowned leaders whom the Prophet chose to represent their tribes. When the first Ansar delegation arrived in Makkah to take the oath of allegiance to the Prophet, Ubadah (may Allah be pleased with him) was one of the 12 believers who pledged allegiance, embraced Islam, and clasped the Prophet's hand in loyalty. In the Second Pledge of Aqabah, Ubadah was one of the leaders of the 70 men and two women who gave his pledge again to the Prophet ﷺ during the Hajj season.

Ever since his pledge, Ubadah never missed a battle or fell short of a sacrifice. After choosing the path of Allah and His Prophet, he dedicated himself to his religious obligations. Therefore, his obedience to Allah and his relationship with his relatives, allies, and enemies were all coloured by his faith.

In the past, Ubadah's family had been allied with the Jews of Medina. After the Prophet ﷺ and his Companions emigrated to Medina, the Jews pretended to be on good terms with them; but after the Battle of Badr (and a little while before the Battle of Uhud), the Medinan Jews began to show their true affiliations. One of the Jewish tribes, Banu Qainuqa, began fabricating reasons to cause strife against the Muslims. As soon as Ubadah realised their real intention, he threw aside their ancient treaty and said, "I take Allah, His Prophet, and those who have believed in Him as my protectors." The Quran descended on the Prophet ﷺ in praise of Ubadah's loyalty saying, *And whosoever takes Allah, His Messenger, and those who have believed as Protectors, then the party of Allah toil be victorious.* (5:56)

Thus, this glorious verse announced the establishment of Allah's party, a party of believers who stood by the Prophet's side, under the banner of guidance and truth. They were regarded as the blossom of a seed sown by their predecessors, who did their utmost to support their Messenger and invite people to believe in Allah. This newly born party of Allah would not only include the Companions of the Prophet ﷺ, but also encompass the true believers of all future generations. Ubadah, whose faithful attitude the verse praised, was not only a representative of the Al-Khazraj tribe, but was also one of the leaders of the righteous Muslims. All of these individuals were a beacon of chivalry and discipline, and an example that continues to inspire today.

One day, Ubadah heard the Prophet ﷺ talking about the responsibilities and obligations of commanders and governors. He spoke of the punishment that awaited any one of them if they abused that authority, or manipulated the money entrusted to them. Muhammad's words shook him so intensely that he swore never to accept command, even over two people. He kept this oath. When the Commander of the Faithful, Umar ibn Al-Khattab (may Allah be pleased with him) became the Caliph, he could not prevail on Ubadah to accept any influential position, except for educating the people in the way of Islam. Indeed, this was the appropriate field for Ubadah, away from influential positions that might jeopardise his faith with precarious arrogance, power, and wealth.

Therefore, Ubadah travelled with Muad ibn Jabal and Abu Ad-Darda to fulfil his new role in Syria. There, they enlightened the country with knowledge and fiqh. Afterward, Ubadah travelled to Palestine, where Muawiyah held jurisdiction in the name of the Caliph. When Ubadah ibn As-Samit finally settled down in Syria, he still considered Medina as the capital of Islam and as the centre of the caliphate. His next home was Palestine, where Muawiyah ibn Abu Sufyan, a worldly-minded and a power-hungry man, ruled.

Ubadah was, indeed, one of those blessed men who lived the most accomplished of their days with the Prophet ﷺ. Ubadah had embraced Islam out of conviction rather than fear. Indeed, he sold himself and his fortune to Allah. He was one of the few men who were nurtured and disciplined by Muhammad ﷺ, who were infused with his wisdom and enlightenment. To Ubadah, one of the most excellent role models of men in power was Umar. Naturally, if Ubadah tried to judge Muawiyah's conduct and character according to those standards, the result would not be in his favour and conflict would be inevitable. And that is exactly what happened.

Ubadah used to say, "We have given a pledge to the Prophet ﷺ to never to be afraid of anyone but Allah." Ubadah was a man who kept his pledges; therefore, he never feared Muawiyah. Although Muawiyah was in authority, Ubadah had already taken oath to stand fast and to expose his wrongdoings.

Consequently, the people of Palestine watched him closely, waiting with baited breath for news of a fearless opposition led by Ubadah. Notwithstanding the patience that Muawiyah was famous for, he soon got tired of Ubadah's opposition and he eventually considered it a direct threat to his authority. When Ubadah realised that the gap between him and Muawiyah was becoming ever wider, he addressed Muawiyah saying, "By Allah, I will never live in the same land with a man like you." Consequently, he left Palestine and returned to Medina.

Umar had been careful to surround governors like Muawiyah with a group of pious and steadfast advisers. He had hoped to curb the aspiration and avarice of such governors by reminding them of the Prophet's era through these ascetic Companions. Therefore, no sooner had Umar seen Ubadah in Medina than he asked him, "What brought you back to Medina?" When Ubadah told him about his dispute with Muawiyah, he ordered him, "Go back to where you belong. By Allah, any land that has no one like you living in it is a wasteland."

Umar immediately sent a message to Muawiyah saying, "You are not to rule over Ubadah." Indeed, Ubadah was a commander in and of himself. When a man like Umar held Ubadah in such high regard, then he was undoubtedly a worthy man. Ubadah's greatness was unveiled through his faith, conscientiousness, and discipline.

This sensible representative of the Ansar and Islam died in 34 AH, and his memory will forever be honoured by the Muslims.

(16)

KHABBAB IBN AL-ARAT

A MASTER IN THE ART OF SELF–SACRIFICE

One day, a group from the Quraysh hastened to Khabbab's house to collect the swords they had asked him to make. Khabbab was a sword maker who sold his wares to the people of Makkah or sent them to market. It was not like Khabbab to leave his house and work; therefore, the Quraysh sat there and waited for his return.

After a long time, Khabbab arrived. His face was bright with questions, and his eyes were filled with tears. He immediately greeted his guests and sat down. They asked him in a hurry, "Khabbab, did you finish making our swords?" Now his eyes filled with delight, and he said, as if to himself, "It makes me wonder!" His clients asked him, "What makes you wonder? We ask you about our swords. Did you finish them?" Khabbab gazed at them as if in a trance. Then he asked them, "Did you see him? Did you hear him?" They looked at one another in astonishment. Then one of them asked slyly, "Did *you* see him Khabbab?" Khabbab asked, "Whom do you mean?" turning the tables back on him. The man answered, irritated, "I mean the same person that you mean!"

Khabbab was careful in his answer. If he were to confess his faith, he would rather announce it in public - not be duped or led on to do otherwise. But, he was still in a state of spiritual upliftment, when he answered, "Yes, I did see and hear him. As a matter of fact, I have seen him enveloped and illuminated by truth."

Suddenly, the Quraysh clients began to realise what he meant. One of them shouted, "Who are you talking about, you slave of Umm Ammar?" Khabbab answered quietly, "Who else but the Arab brother? Who else of your people is enveloped and illuminated by truth?" Another shouted and jumped back in terror, "Do you mean Muhammad?" Khabbab nodded in satisfaction and said, "Yes, he is the Messenger of Allah to us, to bring us out of the darkness of disbelief into the light of belief."

No sooner had he finished these words than he fell unconscious. The only thing he remembered was waking up after many hours to find his clients gone and his body full of bleeding bruises and wounds. Nevertheless, his wide eyes took in his surroundings as if seeing the world anew. Despite the pain, he rose and limped out of the house.

His eyes searched the horizon, engulfed in sublime contemplation and deep thought. Then he returned home to treat his wounds and prepare himself for a new type of torture. From that day, Khabbab was constantly oppressed and abused. Despite his poverty and weakness, he still rose up against the Quraysh's haughtiness and tyranny.

That time heralded the end of an era of paganism and despotism; and announced the dawn of a new world. A world where Allah was Sovereign, worshipped alone by people who obey Him and do righteous deeds sincerely for His sake. Moreover, it announced glad tidings for the weak and oppressed, who stood up as one under the standard of Islam. They would finally stand on equal terms with those who used and abused them in the past.

Khabbab withstood the consequences that ensued after embracing Islam with exceptional courage. Ash-Shabi narrated, "Khabbab withstood all the horrors that the polytheists exposed him too. They went so far as to place burning stones onto his naked back until his flesh came off." Indeed, Khabbab had his share of cruel torture, but his resistance and patience were extraordinary. For instance, the polytheists of the Quraysh turned all the iron they could find in Khabbab's place - which he had used to make swords - into fetters and chains. They put them under the fire until they blazed, then chained his body, hands, and legs with them.

Such was their oppression, that Khabbab and some of his abused brethren asked the Prophet ﷺ one day to help them, instead he reminded them of the sacrifices that came before them. Khabbab himself narrates the story: "One day, we went to the Prophet and found him laying his head on a garment in the shade of the Kaba, so we said to him, 'O Messenger of Allah, we hope that you will ask Allah to bestow His victory and safety on us'. Instantly, the Prophet sat up, and his face reddened as he said, 'Not a long time ago, men like you who believed in Allah used to be dragged into a ditch where they were sawed from the head downwards, yet this didn't make them turn back from their religion. They also used to comb them with iron combs that split their flesh and bones, yet they didn't turn their backs on their religion. Believe me, Allah will put an end to all your sufferings and grant you victory so much so that one day, a man will travel from Sana to Hadramawt and fear no one but Allah and the wolf, lest it should devour his sheep. But you have no patience.'"

As soon as Khabbab and his companions heard these words, they found a new kind of inner determination. They resolved to show Allah and the Prophet ﷺ nothing but patience and self-sacrifice.

The Quraysh were maddened by Khabbab's newfound steadfastness and endurance. So, they decided to seek the help of his former slave mistress, Umm Ammar, who became Khabbab's principal torturer. His new oppressor used to place a burning iron on Khabbab's head to torture him, but Khabbab deliberately controlled himself so as to deprive his torturer of the joy of hearing him moan. One day, the Prophet ﷺ saw his head burned and blackened by the hot iron. His heart was full of sympathy and anguish, and so he did the only thing he could do at that time; he supplicated for him personally: "Allah, make Khabbab victorious over the disbelieving people."

Allah answered this prayer only a few days later. The sweetest recompense befell Umm Ammar, and it was as if an ultimatum had been given to all the torturing she carried out. She suffered a peculiar and acute rabies attack that made her, according to historians, bark like a dog. She was told that the only cure for her ordeal was to cauterize her head. And so, her own head was burned with a red-hot iron, day and night.

———.o.———

All in all, the Quraysh fought faith with torture, while the believers fought torture with self-sacrifice. Not only had Khabbab (may Allah be pleased with him) devoted his time to the service of the new religion, but he also focused on his own worship and instructing others. He used to visit his brothers who hid their Islam in dread of the Quraysh's tyranny and despotism. There, he used to read the Quran and instruct them. He had personally studied every surah and verse of the Quran. Even Abdullah ibn Masud, whom the Prophet praised by saying, "He who wants to read the Quran in exactly the same way it descended on me, should imitate Ibn Umm Abd", considered Khabbab as a reference to all that concerns the Quran.

It was Khabbab who was teaching Quran to Fatima bint Al-Khattab and her husband Sa'id ibn Zaid, when Umar ibn Al-Khattab thrust his way into their house, sword unsheathed. He had come to settle his account with Islam and the Prophet ﷺ. But, Allah willed it so that the moment Umar heard Khabbab reciting a verse from the Quran in a slow and pleasant voice, he instead cried out, "Tell me where Muhammad is!" When Khabbab heard Umar's words, he came out of his hiding place and said, "Umar, by Allah, I do hope that Allah chose you to fulfil the Prophet's supplication. For yesterday, I heard the Prophet say, 'Allah, please support Islam with whom You love best, either Abu Al-Hakam ibn Hisham or Umar ibn Al- Khattab.'" Umar repeated his question, "Where is Muhammad now?" Khabbab answered, "At As-Safa in Dar Al-Arqam ibn Abu Arqam." At that very moment, Umar departed for his blessed destiny.

Khabbab witnessed all the battles and wars of Islam, side by side with the Prophet ﷺ. He treasured his faith throughout his life. When the Bait Al-Mal overflowed with money during the caliphates of Umar and Uthman (may Allah be pleased with them both), Khabbab had a large salary as one of the foremost Muhajirun. This abundant income enabled Khabbab to build himself a house in Kufa. Nevertheless, whenever the Prophet ﷺ and the Companions (who sacrificed their lives for Allah before the Muslims became victorious and wealthy) were mentioned, his eyes filled with tears and he became restless.

Let us listen to Khabbab talking to his brothers who came to visit him on his deathbed...They said, "Be content, Abu Abdullah; you will meet your brothers tomorrow." His eyes flowed with tears as he answered, "I am crying not out of fear of death, but you reminded me of the brothers who left this life without enjoying any of its splendour or luxury, yet we have lived on until we have consumed its splendour and wealth to the extent that we placed this wealth on the sand," and he pointed to his newly-built, humble house. Then he pointed to the place where he kept his money and exclaimed, "By Allah, I have never refused to give it to anyone who asked me for it, as if the strings were his." Then he looked upon his shroud and said weeping, "Look, this is my shroud." He considered it extravagant and luxurious. He then said, "Yet Hamza the Prophet's uncle, on the day of his martyrdom had nothing to be used for a shroud but a torn garment, which if placed on his head, would show his feet, and if placed on his feet, would show his head."

Khabbab was one of the group of believers who the Quranic revelations directly defended once, when the Quraysh's elite asked the Prophet to leave the huddle of poor Muslims around him (that included Khabbab, Suhaib and Bilal) so that they could approach and speak with him. Instead, however, the great Quran glorified those humble men, and these verses descended on the noble Prophet: *[And do not send away those who invoke their Lord, morning and afternoon, seeking His countenance. You are accountable for them in nothing, and they are accountable for you in nothing. So, if you were to send them away you would [then] be of the wrongdoers. And thus, We have tried some of them through others that the disbelievers might say: "Is it these (poor believers) that Allah has favoured from amongst us?" Does not Allah know best those who are grateful?" When those who believe in our verses come to you, say: "Peace be upon you; your Lord has written Mercy for Himself..."]* (6:52-54)

Thus, whenever the Prophet saw them after the revelation of these verses, he took special care to honour them. So much so in fact, that he would spread out his garment for them to sit on next to him, and patted them on their shoulders saying, "I welcome you whom Allah enjoined me to favour." It was indeed a tragic loss when one of the pious, noble, and legitimate sons of revelation and that generation died.

Khabbab, the master of self-denial and sacrifice, passed away in 37 AH. All in all, perhaps the best farewell to Khabbab were in the words of Imam Ali (may Allah be pleased with him) when he was on his way back from Siffin. He saw a recently dug grave and asked about the deceased. They answered, "It is Khabbab's grave." Then he contemplated sorrowfully, "O Allah, bestow Your mercy on Khabbab, for You know that he was a true Muslim, an obedient Muhajir and a determined Mujahid who strove hard in the cause of Allah."

(17)

ABU UBAIDAH IBN AL-JARRAH

The Trustworthy of This Nation

The Prophet ﷺ once held Abu Ubaidah's right hand and said, "In every nation there exists a man worthy of all trust, and the trustworthy of this nation is Abu Ubaidah ibn Al-Jarrah." But who was this man? Who was the man who the Prophet sent with reinforcements in the Dhat As-Salasil Expedition, and who he made commander of the army there - an army included Umar and Abu Bakr amongst its ranks? Who was this Companion who was the first to be called the 'Commander of the Commanders'? Who was that strong, trustworthy man about whom Umar ibn Al- Khattab said on his deathbed, "If Abu Ubaidah ibn Al-Jarrah were alive, I would have entrusted him with the caliphate, and if Allah asked me about him, I would say, I assigned the caliphate to the trustworthy of Allah and His Prophet, Abu Ubaidah Ibn Al- Jarrah."? Let us discover more about Abu Ubaidah.

He embraced Islam at the hands of Abu Bakr Al-Siddiq at the dawn of Islam. He emigrated to Abyssinia during the second emigration, then returned to stand by the Prophet ﷺ at Badr, Uhud, and the rest of the great battles. Even after the Prophet's death, he continued to strive for the sake of Islam during the caliphates of Abu Bakr and Umar. He renounced the world and endured its hardships. He pursued his Islam with an admirable asceticism, piety and firmness. When Abu Ubaidah took the oath of allegiance to the Messenger and dedicated his life in the way of Allah, he truly lived by Allah's guidance. Moreover, he was ready to endure whatever Allah's cause required in self-sacrifice and self-denial.

From the time he shook hands with the Prophet ﷺ as a sign of his pledge, he looked upon himself and his life as something that Allah had entrusted to him. He sought only to gain Allah's pleasure and abandoned every desire or fear that might have distracted him from His path. When Abu Ubaidah fulfilled his pledge, as other Companions did, the Prophet saw in his lifestyle that which made him worthy of the epithet he gave him: 'The Trustworthy of This Nation'.

───── .◦. ─────

Abu Ubaidah's commitment towards his responsibilities was one of his most outstanding traits. For instance, in the Battle of Uhud, he realised from the way the battle was conducted that the disbelievers' first priority was to kill the great Messenger ﷺ. To them, achieving victory was of secondary importance compared to killing the Prophet. Therefore, he decided to stay very close to where he was.

Abu Ubaidah repeatedly thrust his sword into the pagan army that craved to put out the light of Allah once and for all. Whenever the fierce fight led him away from the Prophet, he fought back ferociously, eyes fixed on the Prophet, watching him with great concern. Whenever Abu Ubaidah saw a potential danger approaching the Prophet ﷺ, he jumped swiftly to send the enemies of Allah on their heels before they could injure him.

When the fight reached the height of ferocity, a group of disbelievers closed in upon Abu Ubaidah. Still his eyes were fixed on the Prophet like a hawk. Abu Ubaidah lost his self-control when he saw an arrow hit the Prophet; yet he recollected himself and somehow thrust his sword into those who closed in upon him. Finally, he managed to disperse them and darted towards the Messenger, who was wiping the noble blood that ran down his face with his right hand, then exclaimed, "How can they succeed after they tinged with blood the face of their Prophet who invites them to the way of Allah?"

When Abu Ubaidah saw the two rings of the Prophet's chain mail that had pierced his cheeks, he rushed and held the first one with his front teeth and pulled it out. Yet as it fell, it took out his upper front teeth as well, and the same thing happened to the lower front teeth when he pulled out the second ring.

Abu Bakr Al-Siddiq narrated this incident in more detail: "When the Battle of Uhud reached the apex of fierceness and ferocity, the Prophet was wounded, and two of the rings of the Prophet's mail penetrated his cheeks. As soon as I realised what had happened, I rushed to him. A man ran swiftly in the same direction and exclaimed, 'Dear Allah, accept this deed as a sign of obedience.' Then we both reached the Prophet, but Abu Ubaidah was there before me, so he pleaded with me, 'Please, by Allah, Abu Bakr, let me pull them out of the Prophet's cheeks,' so I let him. Abu Ubaidah held one of the rings with his front teeth and pulled it out along with his upper front teeth. Then he pulled out the second along with his lower front teeth. Thus, he lost his teeth."

Abu Ubaidah, like all the Companions, fulfilled his responsibilities and obligations with great earnestness. Accordingly, when the Prophet ﷺ appointed him as a commander in the Al-Khabat Expedition, he had no supplies except for a knapsack full of dates. Notwithstanding the difficult mission and long distance, Abu Ubaidah withstood all the odds. He and his soldiers marched for miles with nothing to eat but a few dates daily until they ran out. They were forced to pick up withered leaves with their bows, then crush and swallow them with water. Hence, the expedition was called Al-Khabat ('The Struggle'). They proceeded regardless of the danger and the risks. They did not worry about starvation or deprivation. The only thing that mattered to them was to accomplish their glorious mission under the leadership of their strong commander.

———·o·———

The Prophet ﷺ loved this trustworthy man so much that he gave him preference over everyone else. For instance, when the Najran delegation arrived from Yemen after they had embraced Islam, they asked the Prophet to send someone to them to teach them the Quran, the Sunnah, and Islam. The Prophet told them, "I will send you a trustworthy man, a very trustworthy man." When the Companions heard this praise, every one of them prayed that the Prophet was talking about them.

Umar ibn Al-Khattab narrated thus: "I have never craved command in my life except on that day, in hope that I would be the man whom the Prophet held in such high esteem. Therefore, I went in intense heat to perform my Dhuhr prayer. When the Prophet finished leading the prayer, he looked to his right, then to his left. I stood on my toes to draw his attention to me, yet he kept on looking round until he saw Abu Ubaidah ibn Al-Jarrah and ordered him, 'Go with them and judge in truth between them in the matters in which they dispute.' Afterwards, Abu Ubaidah travelled with them."

This incident does not mean that Abu Ubaidah was the only one whom the Prophet trusted or appreciated. He was one of the Companions who equally shared the Prophet's invaluable trust and generous appreciation. But, he was the only one, or one of few, who was qualified to be absent from Medina for this dawah mission, and he was the perfect man for this assignment. He maintained his trustworthiness as a Companion of the Prophet, and even after his death, he upheld his responsibilities with admirable integrity.

He adhered to the standard of Islam wherever he went; both as a soldier in command with valour and esteem, and as a soldier under command with modesty and faithfulness. When Umar ibn Al-Khattab was newly appointed Caliph, his first action was to replace Khalid ibn Al-Walid as the commander of the Muslim armies with Abu Ubaidah.

Abu Ubaidah received notice of his appointment in the midst of a decisive battle, and so he decided to conceal its purport. He pleaded with the messenger to keep it a secret – a sign of his intelligence and fidelity. When Khalid achieved his great victory, and only then, did Abu Ubaidah relay the message to him with extraordinary politeness. On reading the message Khalid asked him, "May Allah bestow His mercy on you, Abu Ubaidah. What made you keep that message from me?" The Trustworthy of the Nation answered, "I was afraid lest it should cause any confusion that might affect the army's morale. We do not crave life or its splendour. We are brothers before Allah."

———•◊•———

Thus, Abu Ubaidah was assigned as the commander-in-chief of Syria. His army was the mightiest and best equipped among the Muslim armies. You could hardly distinguish him from the rank and file of the army. He was always unassuming. When he heard that the people of Syria were infatuated by him and by his new rank, he asked them to assemble, then addressed them saying, "Fellow men, I'm a Muslim from the Quraysh tribe. I will follow any of you like his shadow regardless of the colour of his skin, if he is more pious and righteous than me."

May Allah bless the religion that refined Abu Ubaidah and the Prophet who instructed him! His religion was Islam, and his tribe was Quraysh. For him, this sufficed as an identification. Being the commander-in-chief (the leader of the greatest Muslim army in number, equipment, and victory), and the respected ruler of Syria, were not privileges in themselves. He was not ensnared by the web of conceit or haughtiness. As a matter of fact, all these titles and high positions were just the means to a sublime end.

———•◊•———

One day, the Commander of the Faithful visited Syria and asked those who were at his reception, "Where is my brother?" They asked, "Who do you mean?" He answered, "Abu Ubaidah ibn Al-Jarrah." Soon Abu

Ubaidah arrived, he hugged Umar, then he invited him over to his house, where he had no furniture. In fact, he had nothing but a sword, a shield, and a saddlebag. Umar asked him, smiling, "Why don't you furnish your house as people do?" Abu Ubaidah readily answered, "O Commander of the Faithful, as you see, I have a room to sleep in and that is enough for me."

Some time passed and, one day, as Umar was conducting the affairs of the vast Muslim world, he received the sad news of Abu Ubaidah's death. He tried to control himself, but his sadness got the better of him and his tears flowed. He asked Allah to bestow His mercy on his brother. He recalled his memories with Abu Ubaidah (may Allah be pleased with him) with patience and tenderness. He exclaimed, "If I were to make a wish, I would have wished a house full of men just like Abu Ubaidah."

The Trustworthy of the nation died in the land which he had purified from the paganism of the Persians and the oppression of the Romans. Today, in Jordan, lie his noble remains which once were full of life, goodness, and contentment.

(18)

UTHMAN IBN MADHUN

A 'Monk' Whose Hermitage was Life

If you attempted to arrange the Prophet's Companions in the order that they embraced Islam, Uthman ibn Madhun would be number 14. Not only was he the first Muhajir to die in Medina, but he was also the first Muslim to be buried in Al-Baqi cemetery. This glorious Companion was something of a 'monk'. By monk, we mean a lifelong worshipper, not a monk sequestered in his hermitage; for life with all its commotion, burdens, and virtues was indeed his hermitage. Life to him meant perseverance in the way of in the way of truth and unremitting self-denial and righteousness.

―――――・◇・―――――

Uthman ibn Madhun was there at the dawn of Islam, when the Prophet's words were still spoken in quiet seclusion. He was one of the few who rushed to the way of Allah and supported the Prophet ﷺ. When the Prophet ordered the few oppressed believers to emigrate to Abyssinia, Uthman headed up the first group of fugitives, accompanied by his son, As-Saib.

―――――・◇・―――――

Like the rest of the emigrants to Abyssinia, Uthman ibn Madhun's move away from the Prophet ﷺ only made him hold more firmly to his Islam. The two emigrations to Abyssinia represented a unique and glorious phenomenon in the cause of Islam, for those who believed in Muhammad ﷺ and followed the light that had been sent down to him, had had enough of paganism, error, and ignorance. Their common sense shunned the idolatry of statues made of rocks and clay. When these fugitives emigrated to Abyssinia, they found an already prevalent and highly disciplined religion, with an established clerical hierarchy of bishops and priests. Notwithstanding their attitude towards this religion, it was definitely far from the familiar paganism practiced back home and the usual idolatrous rites left behind. Undoubtedly, the clergy in Abyssinia exerted much effort to lure those emigrants to apostatise and embrace Christianity.

In spite of all this, those emigrants stood steadfast in their profound loyalty to Islam and to the Prophet Muhammad ﷺ. They anxiously yearned for the day when they would return to their beloved country. They longed to worship Allah and support the great Prophet ﷺ in the mosque in peacetime; and to take up arms when the power of disbelief forced them to take up arms in the battlefield. Thus, those emigrants who lived in Abyssinia felt secure and peaceful. Uthman ibn Madhun was one of them, yet his expatriation did not make him forget his cousin Umaiyah ibn Khalaf's plots and the abuse he dealt him and other Muslims. Hence, he used to amuse himself by rehearsing threats to him, saying, "I hope that all the arrows you aim will miss their target and strike back at you. You fought against generous and noble people and tortured them to death. You will soon be punished, and the common people you used to despise will get back at you."

Despite their exile, the emigrants were consumed by their worship of Allah and the study of the Quran. But suddenly, news spread that the Quraysh had submitted themselves to Islam. So, the emigrants quickly packed up their belongings and hastened to return to Makkah. However, no sooner had they reached the city's outskirts than they realised that the news was false, and just a bait to lure them back. They realised that their excessive credulity had led them right into this trap, yet there was nothing they could do.

At that time, the right of protection and refuge was a sacred and honoured Arab tradition. Consequently, if a weak man had a claim on a man of high standing, he would instantly enjoy the privileges of the right of protection. Naturally, not all of those who returned to Makkah had claims on such high-ranking men. Therefore, few enjoyed the protection and safety guaranteed by this right. Among those who did though was Uthman ibn Madhun, who had a claim on Al Walid ibn Al-Mughirah. And so, he entered Makkah safely, and was able to attend its councils without being humiliated or harmed.

Let us not forget though that Ibn Madhun was a man who had been refined by the teachings of the Quran and the discipline of the Prophet ﷺ. Wherever he looked, he saw his weaker Muslim brothers (who had no claim to protection) being atrociously abused. All the while, he sat safe and sound in his sanctuary away from the least provocation. His free spirit rebelled and his noble compassion got the better of him. Therefore, he decided to throw aside Al-Walid's patronage. He left behind his burdensome sanctuary, that he felt was depriving him from receiving more favour from Allah. And in doing so, he followed his persecuted Muslim brothers, an eyewitness narrates what occurred as follows:

"When Uthman ibn Madhun saw the affliction that had befallen the Prophet's Companions while he was free and safe under Al-Walid ibn Al-Mughirah's protection, he said to himself, 'By Allah, I realise now that I have a fatal flaw in my character, for here I am sound under the protection of a disbeliever while my brothers and companions are being abused and tortured by disbelievers.' Instantly, he hastened to Al-Walid ibn Al-Mughirah and spoke, 'Abu Abd Shams, you have been a dutiful friend, you did your utmost to honour the ties of kinship. But now I must forsake my claim on you.' Al-Walid asked him, 'Why, nephew? Did any of my people lay a finger on you?' He answered, 'No, but I'm fully satisfied with Allah's protection and sanctuary and I do not want to resort to anyone but Him. So please come with me to the mosque and withdraw your protection and support in public.' They both hastened to the mosque. Then Al-Walid cried out, 'Uthman has asked me to withdraw my protection and support from him.' Uthman said, 'He was indeed a loyal, dutiful, and generous patron, but I do not like to resort to the protection and help of anyone but Allah.'

'As Uthman was leaving, Lubaid ibn Rabufah was sitting in one of the Quraysh's meetings reciting poetry, so he decided to join them and sat down and heard Lubaid recite, 'Everything but Allah is falsehood.' Uthman nodded and said, 'You spoke the truth.' Lubaid continued, 'Every blessing is transient.' Uthman objected saying, 'You are a liar, for the blessings of Paradise are eternal.' Lubaid said, 'O you Quraysh, by Allah, I have not heard before that anyone dared to call a man, who was attending your meeting, names.' A man of Quraysh explained, 'Do not pay attention to what he says, for he is a fool who has turned apostate.' Uthman objected to the man's insult and both quarrelled until the man lost his temper and punched Uthman's eye ruthlessly.

'Nearby was Al-Walid ibn Al-Mughirah, who saw what had happened and said, 'By Allah, nephew, you could have spared yourself the pain if you had stayed under my invulnerable protection.' Uthman answered, 'On the contrary, my healthy eye yearns for the pain of my abused eye. I am under the protection of Allah, Who is far better and more capable than you, Abu Abd Shams.' Al-Walid urged him saying, 'Come on nephew, be sensible and

return to my sanctuary and protection.' Ibn Madhun said firmly, 'No.' After he left, the pain in his eye was severe yet his spirit was revived, strengthened, and reassured. On his way home he recited, 'I don't care if a deluded disbeliever hurt my eye, for it was in the way of Allah. For the Most Merciful will reward me on the Day of Reckoning in compensation for it. My people, if Allah attempts to please someone, then he will be undoubtedly a happy man. Even if you say that I'm a misguided fool, my life will always be consecrated to the Prophet Muhammad's religion ﷺ. I will always do my utmost to please Allah, for our religion is the only truth despite abuse and oppression'."

In this way, Uthman set the best of examples and his graceful words continue to resonate till this day: "By Allah, my healthy eye yearns to be hurt in the way of Allah. I am under the protection and care of Someone far better and more capable than you." Obviously Uthman's abuse at the hands of the Quraysh was now inevitable; he provoked it and was in fact ready to receive it, for this abuse was to him like a fire that purifies and ennobles faith.

Some time later, Uthman decided to emigrate to Medina where he would not be harassed by the like of Abu Jahl, Abu Lahab, Umaiyah, Utbah, or indeed any of the other ruthless people who abused and tormented the Muslims. He travelled to Medina alongside other great Companions who had survived similar hardships with admirable steadfastness. They did not, however, emigrate to Medina to rest. On the contrary, Medina was the springboard that enabled Muslims to strive in the way of Allah all over the world, and cling to His cause by spreading His guidance.

When Uthman had settled in the illuminated city of Medina, his remarkable qualities were finally unveiled. He emerged as an ascetic, devout, and repentant worshipper. He spent his life striving in the way of Allah: worshipper by night and fighter by day.

Although all the Prophet's ﷺ Companions at that time were inclined to asceticism and devoutness, Ibn Madhun had a certain strategy that was specific to him. He was so remarkably absorbed in his devoutness that he turned his life, day and night, into a perpetual state of prayer and glorification. No sooner had he sipped the sweet engrossment of worship than he hastened to abandon all the enticing luxury of life.

Henceforth, he wore nothing but coarse clothes and ate nothing but the simplest of food.

One day, he walked into the mosque in which the Prophet ﷺ and his Companions were sitting, and he had on a faded, worn-out garment that was patched with a piece of fur. As soon as the Prophet saw him, he sympathised with him, and the Companions' eyes were filled with tears, yet the Prophet ﷺ said, "Would you like it if you were rich enough to have as many garments as you like and as much food as you like? Would you like your upholstery to be as expensive as the clothes used in covering the Kaba?" The Companions answered, "We would indeed! We would like to live in luxury surrounded by the splendours of life." The Prophet ﷺ commented, "You will be wealthy, but you are today far better in your piety and devoutness than you will be when you are wealthy." Naturally, when Ibn Madhun heard the Prophet's words, he clung even more to his austere life. He went so far as to renounce intercourse with his wife, yet when the Prophet ﷺ heard about this exaggerated approach, he summoned him and said, "Your wife has the right to have relations with you."

As a Companion, the Prophet ﷺ loved Uthman dearly. When his pure spirit embarked on its journey towards Heaven, the Prophet was by his side, paying his last farewell to the first Muhajir to die in Medina, and the first to be raised to Paradise. He leaned to kiss his forehead and his amiable eyes filled with tears that wet Uthman's face. The Prophet ﷺ bid farewell to his beloved Companion by saying, "Allah bestow His mercy on you, Abu As-Saib. You are now leaving life that was not able to seduce or mislead you."

The revered Prophet ﷺ did not forget his Companion after his death; on the contrary, he often mentioned and praised him. For instance, his very last words to his daughter Ruqayyah on her deathbed were, "Go on, follow in the pious and devout Uthman ibn Madhun's footsteps up to Paradise."

(19)

ZAID IBN HARITHA

The Beloved

At the Battle of Mu`tah, the Prophet ﷺ stood to pay his farewell to the departing Muslim army on its way to fight the Romans. He announced the names of the three successive commanders of the army: "Zaid ibn Haritha is your first commander, but in case he is wounded, Jafar ibn Abu Talib will take over the command, and if the latter is wounded then Abdullah ibn Rawahah will replace him." But who was this first commander, Zaid ibn Haritha – fondly known as 'The Beloved' of the Prophet ﷺ?

Let us return to a time when Haritha, Zaid's father, was loading a camel with luggage to send his wife, Sudah, to her family. Haritha bid farewell to his wife who carried Zaid, their young child, in her arms. And yet, every time he sought to leave his wife and child to their caravan, to return to his house and work, he felt the inexplicable urge to keep his wife and son in sight. Sadly though the time had come for them to set off. Haritha paid his last farewell to his wife and son, and headed home. His tears flowed as he said goodbye and he stood pinned to the spot until he lost sight of them. At that moment, he was heartbroken.

Sudah stayed with her family for a while. One day, suddenly her neighbourhood was attacked by one of its opposing tribes. Taken by surprise, Banu Ma'n were defeated and Zaid ibn Haritha was captured along with other war prisoners. His mother returned home alone. When Haritha heard the sad news, he was thunderstruck. He travelled everywhere and asked everyone about his beloved Zaid. He recited these lines of poetry on the spur of the moment to lament the loss of his son:

> *My heart was broken when I lost Zaid.*
> *I don't know if he is alive or dead or if I will ever see him again.*
> *By Allah, I still do not know if he was killed on the plain or slain on the mountain.*
> *His picture comes to the mind's eye whenever the sun rises or sets.*
> *Even when the wind blows, it brings along his memory.*
> *Alas, I am shrouded by my sadness, grief, and fear for him.*

At that time, slavery was a recognised and established social fact, even a necessity. This was the case in Athens, Rome, and indeed throughout the ancient world, including the Arab Peninsula. When the opposing tribe attacked the Banu Ma`n, it headed to the market of Ukadh, where prisoners of war were sold. There, Zaid was sold to Hakim ibn Huzam, who gave him to his aunt Khadija as a gift. At that time, Khadija was married to Muhammad ibn Abdullah but the revelation had not yet descended on him. Khadija gave her servant Zaid as a wedding gift to her husband, soon to be Allah's Prophet *My heart was broken*. He was very pleased with Zaid and manumitted him at once to make him a free man. His great and compassionate heart overflowed with care towards the boy.

Later on, during one of the Hajj seasons, a group of Haritha's tribe happened to run into Zaid in Makkah and told him about his parents' anguish ever since they had lost him. Zaid asked them to convey his love and longing to his parents. He told them, "Tell my father that I live here with the most generous and loving father." No sooner did his father know his son's whereabouts, than he hastened on his way to him, accompanied by his brother.

As soon as they reached Makkah, he asked about the trustworthy Muhammad. When he met him, he said, "O son of Ibn Abdul Muttalib! O son of the master of his tribe! Your land is one of security and sanctuary and you are famous for helping the distressed and sheltering the captive. We have come here to ask you to give us back our son. So please confer a favour on us and set a reasonable ransom for him." The Prophet knew the great love and attachment Zaid carried in his heart for him, yet at the same time, he respected Haritha's parental right. Therefore, he told Haritha, "Ask Zaid to come here and make him choose between you and me. If he chooses you, he is free to go with you, but if he chooses me then, by Allah, I will not leave him for anything in the world." Haritha's face brightened, for he did not expect such magnanimity; therefore, he said, "You are far more generous than us." Then the Prophet ﷺ summoned Zaid. When he arrived, he asked him, "Do you recognise these people?" Zaid said, "Yes, this is my father and this is my uncle."

The Prophet ﷺ told him what he had told Haritha. Zaid replied, "I will not choose anyone but you, for you are a father and an uncle to me." The Prophet's eyes were full of thankful and compassionate tears.

He held Zaid's hand and walked to the Kaba, where the Quraysh were holding a meeting, and cried out, "I bear witness that Zaid is my son, and in case I die first, he will inherit from me, and in case he dies first, I will inherit from him." Haritha was content, for not only had his son been freed, but he had also become the son of the man who was known by the Quraysh as 'The Honest and Trustworthy'. Moreover, Muhammad ﷺ was a descendant of Banu Hashim and was raised to a high station among his people, thereby raiding his own son's status.

Zaid's father and uncle returned back home leaving their son safe. He had become his own master, and the Prophet ﷺ had set to rest their fears concerning his fate. The Prophet ﷺ adopted Zaid and from that moment on he was known as Zaid ibn Muhammad.

─────•◊•─────

One bright morning, the revelation suddenly descended on Muhammad ﷺ: *Read! In the name of your Lord who created - created mankind from something which clings; read! And your Lord is the Most Noble; who taught by the pen; taught mankind what he did not know* (96:1-5). Then the revelation continued: *O you covered - Arise and warn! And magnify your Lord.* (74:1-3) And: *O Messenger! Proclaim the message which has been sent down to you from your Lord. And if you do not, then you have not conveyed His message. Allah will protect you from mankind. Verily, Allah guides not the people who disbelieve.* (5:61)

As soon as the Prophet ﷺ had shouldered the responsibility of his message, Zaid submitted himself to Islam. Narrators said that he was the second, or possibly even the first, man to embrace Islam after Muhammad ﷺ.

─────•◊•─────

The Prophet ﷺ loved Zaid so dearly due to Zaid's singular loyalty, conscientiousness and trustworthiness. All this and more, made Zaid ibn Haritha (or 'Zaid, the Beloved One' as the Companions used to call him) hold a distinguished place in the Prophet's heart ﷺ. Aisha (may Allah be pleased with her) said, "The Prophet ﷺ never sent Zaid on an expedition but as a commander, and if his life had not been so short, he would have made him his successor."

Was it possible for anyone to be held in such high esteem by the

Prophet? If so, what was Zaid really like? Above all, Zaid had a compassionate heart and a free soul. He was raised to the highest position by his Islam and by the Prophet's love for him; for neither Islam nor the Prophet ﷺ took notice of descent or prestige. Muslims like Bilal, Suhaib, Khabbab, Ammar, Usama and Zaid were all alike according to this great religion. Each one of them played an important and distinctive role in providing the impetus for the rapid spread of Islam. Islam reset life's values when the glorious Quran decreed: *Surely, the most honourable among you in the sight of Allah are the most pious of you* (49:13). Moreover, it encouraged pure, trustworthy, and productive qualities in people.

The Prophet ﷺ married his cousin Zaynab to Zaid. Sadly, it seems that Zaynab (may Allah be pleased with her) only accepted that offer of marriage because her shyness prevented her from turning down the Prophet's suggestion. Unfortunately, the gap between the couple widened every day, and finally their marriage collapsed. The Prophet ﷺ felt that he was, in a way, responsible for this marriage which ended up in divorce. However, much to her joy, the Prophet himself eventually married his cousin Zaynab himself. He chose a new wife, Umm Kulthum bint Uqbah, for Zaid.

The slanderers and the enemies of the Prophet spread doubt concerning the legality of Muhammad's marriage to his adopted son's ex-wife. However, the Quran directly refuted their claims by striking a distinction between sons and adopted sons. It abrogated adoption altogether saying: *Mohammed is not a father of any man among you, but he is the Messenger of Allah and the last of the Prophets* (33:90). Hence, Zaid was called by his father's name again: Zaid ibn Haritha.

Now, can you imagine the Muslim troops that marched towards the Battle of Al-Jumuh? Their commander was Zaid ibn Haritha. Do you see those Muslims troops that marched to At-Tarf, Al-Is, Hisma and to other battles? The commander of all those battles was Zaid ibn Haritha. Truly, as Aisha already said, "The Prophet never sent Zaid on an expedition but as a commander."

At last, the Battle of Mu'tah took place. It seems that the Romans and their senescent empire were filled with apprehension about the rapid spread of Islam. They saw it as a genuine and fatal threat to their very existence, especially in Syria, which bordered the centre of the new, sweeping religion. Therefore, they used Syria as a springboard to the Arab Peninsula and the Muslim nation.

The Prophet ﷺ realised that the aim of the Roman skirmishes was to test the Muslim combat readiness. Therefore, he decided to take the initiative and exhibit Islam's determination to resist and to gain ultimate victory. On 1st Jumada 8 AH, the Muslim army marched towards Al-Balqa in Syria until they reached its borders, where the Romans army and its allied Arab tribes resided. The Roman army pitched camp at a place called Masharif, and the Muslim army pitched camp near a town called Mu`tah.

The Prophet ﷺ knew how crucial this battle was; therefore, he chose three Companions for its command, all were worshippers by night and fighters by day. Those three fighters sold their lives and property to Allah, and renounced their desires for the sake of great martyrdom to gain Allah's pleasure. These three commanders were in succession: Zaid ibn Haritha, Jafar ibn Abu Talib and Abdullah ibn Rawahah (may Allah be pleased with them all). Thus, the Prophet ﷺ stood to bid farewell to his army and gave them his order we have already heard: "Zaid ibn Haritha is your first commander, but in case he is wounded, Jafar ibn Abu Talib will take over the command, and if he is also wounded, Abdullah ibn Rawahah will take over."

Although Jafar ibn Abu Talib was one of the Prophet's closest friends who had valour and good lineage, the Prophet still chose him as the second in command after Zaid. In doing so, the Prophet ﷺ emphasised the fact that Islam came to abolish superficial discrimination. Instead, it established a new respect for merit, and merit alone.

It was as if the Prophet foresaw the proceedings of the imminent battle, for he assigned the command of the army to Zaid, Jafar, and then Abdullah and strangely enough, all of them were raised to Allah in the same order set by him. When the Muslims saw the vanguard of the Roman army, which they had estimated at 200,000 warriors, they were stunned by its enormity. But since when did the battles of faith depend on number?

At that moment, the Muslims flung themselves into the battlefield regardless of the consequences. Their commander, Zaid, carried the Prophet's standard and fought his way through the enemy's spears, arrows, and swords. Zaid saw neither the sand of Al-Balqa, nor the Roman forces. The only things that he saw were the hills of Paradise and its green abundance that awaited him. When he thrust his sword, he not only struck at the necks of his enemies, but he also flung the doors open to the eternal abode of peace and Allah's company. Zaid clung to his destiny. As he finally ascended to the heavens, Zaid's spirit must have smiled serenely on seeing his second in command, Jafar, dart towards the standard and hold it high before it even touched the ground.

(20)

JAFAR IBN ABU TALIB

Most Like Muhammad ﷺ in Looks and Conduct

Jafar was known for his many good qualities. He possessed an inimitable youth, unending patience, compassion, piety and modesty. He was known for his fearlessness, generosity, chastity and trustworthiness. Do not let the fact that all these traits were found in one man astonish you, for you are looking at a man who resembled the Prophet ﷺ in both looks and conduct. The Prophet gave him the epithet 'Father of the Poor' and the agnomen 'The Two Winged'. You are about to find out why, when you meet the beloved Jafar ibn Abu Talib - one of the great Muslims who contributed much to the shaping of the Islamic conscience.

He was among the early believers who embraced Islam, and was raised to a high station in life thereafter. On the same day as Jafar, his wife (Asma bint Umais) also submitted herself to Islam. After their conversion, they had their share of abuse and oppression, which they withstood with courage. When the Prophet ﷺ advised his Companions to emigrate to Abyssinia, Jafar and his wife were among those who acted upon his advice. There, they settled for a number of years, during which they had three children: Muhammad, Abdullah and Awf.

In Abyssinia, Jafar was known as the eloquent Companion who won over others through the way of Allah and His Prophet ﷺ. His noble heart, alert mind, sagacious spirit, and fluent speech were just some of the many graces that Allah bestowed on him. The Battle of Mu'tah, at which he was martyred, was his most magnificent feat. Yet the Day of Al-Mujawarah, an incident which took place before the court of An-Najashi in Abyssinia, was an equally memorable occasion and a battle of words. Let us consider the events of this day in more detail.

The Muslim emigration to Abyssinia did not allay the fears of the Quraysh, nor did it lessen their grudges against the Muslims. On the contrary, the Quraysh were afraid lest the Muslims should gain momentum there, and increase in both number and power. If that did not happen, the Quraysh's arrogance could still not accept the fact that those fugitives had fled their tyranny and had settled in another country, which the Prophet ﷺ saw as a promising land for Islam. Therefore, the Quraysh leaders decided to send delegates to An-Najashi with expensive gifts in the hope that he would expel the Muslims from his country. The two chosen delegates were Abdullah ibn Abu Rabuah and Amr ibn Al-As (this was before they both embraced Islam).

An-Najashi, or the Negus, was the emperor of Abyssinia and an enlightened believer. Deep down, he embraced a rational and pure Christianity - void of deviation or fanaticism. He was renowned and highly admired for his justice. Hence, the Prophet ﷺ chose his country for his Companions' immigration. In the hope of convincing him of their view against the Muslims, the Quraysh delegates brought many expensive gifts for the bishops and archbishops of the church. They were advised not to meet An-Najashi until they had given those presents to the bishops. Their task was to convince them of their position first, so that they would support them when they stood before An-Najashi.

As soon as the two delegates arrived in Abyssinia, they met with the spiritual leaders and lavished their gifts on them. Then they sent An-Najashi his presents. Afterwards, they began to incite the priests and bishops against the Muslim immigrants and asked them to support them in their plea to An-Najashi to expel them. A day was set for the Muslims to meet An-Najashi, so that the Quraysh's representatives could confront their mischievous enemies in front of the Negus.

On the appointed day, An-Najashi sat on his throne with great dignity, surrounded by the bishops and his retinue. In the vast hall in front of him sat the Muslim immigrants, calmed by Allah's tranquillity and mercy. The two Quraysh delegates stood to reiterate their accusations against the Muslims, which they had already presented to An-Najashi in private.

They were reported to have said, "Your Majesty, you well know that a group of fools has turned renegade and have taken asylum in your country. They did not embrace your religion, but rather invented their own religion that neither of us know. We are people of high rank who are related to their fathers, uncles, and tribes, so that you would surrender those wretched renegades to us."

An-Najashi addressed the Muslims saying, "What is that religion that made you abandon your people's religion and refuse to embrace our religion?" Jafar had been chosen by mutual consultation to speak for the Muslims. So, he stood up slowly, and looking on with appreciation towards the hospitable king, he said:

"O your Majesty, we used to be a people of ignorance. We worshipped idols, ate dead animals, committed great sin, severed family relations, and acted according to the law of the jungle. We used to believe that survival was only for the fittest until Allah sent from among us a Prophet ﷺ who was known for his noble descent, honesty, trustworthiness, and chastity. He invited us to worship Allah alone and abstain from worshipping stones and idols. He ordered us to speak nothing but the truth and to render back our trusts to those whom they are due.

'Moreover, he ordered us to keep our ties of kinship intact, be good to our neighbours, and abstain from what is forbidden. He also ordered us not to commit evil, nor to say false statements, nor to eat up the property of orphans, nor to accuse chaste women of wrongdoing without proof or witness. Hence, we believed in him and in Allah's message to him. We worship Allah alone. We rejected that which we used to associate with Him as His partners. We allowed as lawful what is halal and prohibited as unlawful what is haram. Consequently, we were harassed and abused by our people, who tried to turn us away from what Allah had sent down to the Prophet ﷺ so that we may return to idol worshiping and the evil and unlawful deeds we used to do. We were oppressed, abused and straitened in a way that prevented us from the proper worship of Allah. They even tried to force us to turn apostate. Therefore, we fled to your country and asked for asylum to escape oppression and tyranny."

―――――・◇・―――――

When Jafar finished his glorious speech, An-Najashi was overcome with compassion and grace. He addressed Jafar saying, "Do you have a scroll on which you have written the words of your Prophet?" Jafar replied, "Yes." An-Najashi ordered, "Read it aloud." Jafar recited a number of verses from Surah Maryam in such a slow, sweet and captivating voice that it made An-Najashi and his bishops cry.

When he had wiped his tears, he said to the Quraysh delegates,

"These words, of what descended on Isa (Jesus), come from the very same source as that of Isa. You are free men in a free land. By Allah, I will never surrender you to them."

The meeting was over. Allah had helped the Muslims and made their feet firm; whereas the Quraysh delegates were bitterly defeated. But, Amr ibn Al-As was a resourceful man who could neither accept defeat nor despair easily. Therefore, no sooner had he returned to their residence than he sat turning the matter over in his mind. Then he addressed his comrade saying, "By Allah, I will go to An-Najashi tomorrow and I will pluck the Muslims out from this land once and for all." His comrade replied, "You must not do that, for despite their disobedience, they are still related to us." Amr said, "By Allah, I will tell An-Najashi that they claim that Isa ibn Maryam is a slave like the rest of Allah's slaves." Thus, the web was spun by the shrewd delegate so as to lead the Muslims unawares right into a trap. The Muslims were in an awkward position, for if they said that Isa was Allah's slave, they would incite the king and bishops against them. And, if they denied the fact that he was human, then they would be going against their religion.

On the following day, Amr hastened to meet the king and said, "Your Majesty, those Muslims utter an awful saying against Isa." At once, the bishops were agitated by offensive statement. They asked the Muslims once again to meet the king so as to clarify their religious standpoint concerning Isa.

When the Muslims found out about the new plot, they discussed their options, then agreed to say nothing but the truth as said by the Prophet ﷺ, regardless of the consequences. Once again, the audience was held and An-Najashi started it by asking Jafar, "What does your religion say about Isa?" Jafar, stood once again like a beacon of light and said, "We say what has descended on our Prophet ﷺ: he is Allah's slave [and] Messenger, His word which He bestowed, and a spirit created by Him." An-Najashi cried out in assent and said that the same words had been said by Isa to describe himself, but the lines of bishops roared in disapproval. Nevertheless, the enlightened, believing An-Najashi declared, "You are free to go now. My land is your sanctuary. Anyone who dares to abuse or mistreat you in any way will be severely punished." He addressed his retinue and pointed towards the Quraysh's delegation declaring, "Give them back their presents, for I do not want them. By Allah, Allah did not take a bribe from me when He restored my kingdom; therefore, I will not be bribed against Him!"

After the Quraysh delegates had been utterly disgraced, they headed back to Makkah. The Muslims, led by Jafar, went on with their secure lives in Abyssinia. They settled in the "most hospitable land of the most hospitable people" until Allah gave them permission to return to their Prophet ﷺ, who was celebrating with the Muslims the conquest of Khaibar when Jafar and the rest of the emigrants to Abyssinia arrived. The Prophet's ﷺ heart was filled with joy, happiness, and optimism.

The Prophet ﷺ hugged him and said, "I do not know which makes me feel happier, Khaibar's conquest or Jafar's arrival." The Prophet and his Companions travelled to Makkah to perform Umrah and then they returned to Medina. Jafar was overjoyed with the news he heard concerning the heroism and valour of his believing brothers who had fought side by side with the Prophet ﷺ in the Battles of Badr, Uhud and others. His eyes filled with tears over the Companions who had been true to their covenant with Allah, and who had fulfilled their obligations as obedient martyrs. Jafar craved Paradise more than anything in the world. He waited impatiently for the glorious moment in which he would win his own martyrdom.

The Battle of Mu'tah, as we have already mentioned, was imminent. Jafar realised that this battle was his chance to either achieve a glorious victory for Allah's religion or win martyrdom in the way of Allah. Therefore, he pleaded with the Prophet ﷺ to let him fight in this battle. Jafar knew beyond doubt that this battle was not going to be easy, and was in fact a crucial war against the armies of a vast and powerful empire. This empire excelled the Arabs and Muslims in numbers, equipment, expertise, and finance. He yearned to be a part of it.

Thus, he was the second of the three commanders set by Muhammad ﷺ. The two armies met in combat on a stressful day. Jafar would have been forgiven if he had been gripped by terror when he saw the

200,000 warriors. But instead, he was gripped by overflowing exaltation, for he felt urged by the pride of the noble believer and the self-confidence of the hero to fight with his equals.

Again, hardly had the standard touched the sand as it slipped from Zaid ibn Haritha's right hand, when Jafar darted to pick it up. He broke through the line of the enemy with incredible fearlessness. When the Roman warriors finally closed in upon him in an encircling move, his horse restricted his movement, so he dismounted and thrust his sword into his enemies. Then he saw one of them approaching his horse so as to mount it. He did not want this impure disbeliever on his horse's back, so he thrust his sword into it and killed it.

He immediately broke through the encircled Roman warriors like a hurricane and recited these vehement lines of poetry:

> How wonderful Paradise is.
> I can see it approaching with its sweet and cool drink.
> The time for the punishment of the Romans is drawing near.
> Those unbelievers are not related to us in blood.
> I must fight the Romans whenever I see one of their warriors.

The Roman soldiers were stunned by this warrior who fought alone like a fully armoured army. Confounded by his courage, they closed in upon him in a way that left him no escape, for they were determined to slay him. Instantly, they struck with their swords and cut off his right hand. Swiftly he caught the standard with his left hand before it reached the ground. When they struck off his left hand, he caught the standard with his upper arms. At the moment, the only thing that really mattered to him was not to let the standard of the Prophet ﷺ touch the ground as long as he was alive. Although his body was being struck down, his upper arms still hugged the standard close. The sounds of its fluttering must have summoned Abdullah ibn Rawahah, who swiftly took it from the dying arms of Jafar, then galloped towards his own great destiny.

Thus, Jafar died an honourable death. He met Allah, the Most Great, the Most High, clothed in self-sacrifice and heroism. When Allah the All-Knower, the All-Aware, inspired His Prophet ﷺ with the outcome of the battle and Jafar's martyrdom, his tears flowed as he placed his spirit in Allah's hands. He went to his late cousin's house and called his children. He hugged and kissed them as his tears flowed. Then, Muhammad ﷺ went back to his meeting surrounded by the Companions. Hasan ibn Thabut, the poet laureate of Islam, lamented the death of Jafar and his Companions saying:

> *At daybreak a man of a blessed nature and graceful face*
> *Commanded the believers to death.*
> *His face was as bright as the moon.*
> *He was a proud man who descended from Al Hashim.*
> *He was a valiant man who rushed to help the oppressed.*
> *He fought until he was martyred*
> *And his reward was Paradise where there are lush green gardens.*
> *Jafar was loyal and obedient to Muhammad.*
> *If Islam lost one of Al-Hashim,*
> *There are still honourable and pious men of them*
> *Who are the support and pride of Islam.*

After Hasan finished reciting his poem, Kab ibn Malik also recited:

> *I am grief stricken over the group*
> *Who were struck down in succession in the Battle of Mu'tah.*
> *They strived and fought fiercely and didn't turn their back.*
> *Allah sent His blessings on them*
> *For they were pious and loyal men.*
> *Allah made the heavy rains water their bone.*
> *They stood firm before death in Mu'tah*
> *in obedience to Allah*
> *And for fear of His punishment.*
> *They were guided by Jafar's flag. He was the best Commander.*
> *He broke through the line of the enemy*
> *and was struck down*
> *Owing to the fierce and ruthless fight.*
> *Instantly, the bright moon darkened*
> *And the sun eclipsed to lament his death.*

At the end, all the poor wept bitterly over the loss of their 'father', for Jafar was indeed the 'Father of the Poor'. Abu Hurairah said, "The most generous man towards the poor was Jafar ibn Abu Talib." Indeed, even in death, he was a generous and devoted martyr. Abdullah ibn Umar said, "I was with Jafar in the Battle of Mu'tah and we looked around for him. We found that the enemy had sprayed his body with more than 90 stabs and strikes!"

But those killers did not scratch his invulnerable spirit. No, their swords and spears were the bridge by which this martyr crossed to be near Allah, the Most Merciful, the Most High. He was raised to a high station in heaven. His worn-out body was covered all over with his wounds, his own medals of war. The Prophet ﷺ once said of Jafar, "I have seen him in Paradise. His head and wings [upper arms] were covered with blood." And so he descended to his next life as the 'Two Winged' martyr, in memory of his valour at Mu'tah.

(21)

ABDULLAH IBN RAWAHAH

*'O My Soul, Death Is Inevitable, So It Is
Better for You to Be Martyred'*

When the Prophet ﷺ met secretly with a Medinan delegation on the outskirts of Makkah, 12 representatives of the Ansar took an oath of allegiance at the Pledge of Aqabah. Abdullah ibn Rawahah was one of those representatives, all of whom ushered Islam into Medina and paved the way for the hijra, largely considered a springboard for the faith. Abdullah was also one of the 73 of the Ansar who gave the Prophet ﷺ the Second Pledge of Aqabah, in the following year. After the Prophet and his Companions migrated and settled in Medina, Abdullah ibn Rawahah was the most proactive of the Ansar in his attempts to support the thriving religion. He was also the most alert to the plots of Abdullah ibn Ubaiy, whom the people of Medina were about to crown king before the Muslims arrived. Ibn Ubaiy never really got over the bitterness he felt for losing the chance of his lifetime to become a king. And so, he used his craftiness to weave deceitful plots against Islam. Abdullah ibn Rawahah kept a track of his craftiness and frustrated most of Ibn Ubaiy's plots.

Ibn Rawahah (may Allah be pleased with him) was a scribe at a time in which writing was not prevalent. He was also a poet and his poetry flowed with admirable fluency. After embracing Islam, he devoted all his poetic genius to its service. The Prophet ﷺ always admired his poetry, asking him to recite more of it. One day, as he was sitting among his Companions, Abdullah ibn Rawahah joined them, and so the Prophet asked him, "How do you compose a poem?" Abdullah answered, "First I think about its subject matter, then I recite." Then, he immediately recited:

> *O the good descendants of Al Hashim*
> *Allah raised you to a high station*
> *Of which you are worthy above all mankind.*
> *My intuition made me realise at once*
> *Your excelling nature,*
> *Contrary to the disbelievers' belief in you.*
> *If you asked some of them for support and help,*
> *They would turn you down.*
> *May Allah establish the good that descends on you firmly*
> *And bestow victory upon you as He did to Musa.*

The Prophet ﷺ was elated and said, "I hope that Allah will make your feet firm, too." When the Prophet was circumambulating the Kaba in the compensatory Umrah he performed, Ibn Rawahah recited to him,

> *Were it not for Allah, we would not have been*
> *Guided to the Right path nor charitable*
> *Nor able to perform our prayers.*
> *So, descend! Peace of mind and reassurance,*
> *On us and establish our feet firmly*
> *When we meet our enemy*
> *In combat. If our oppressors tried to spread*
> *Affliction and trial, unrest, among us*
> *We will not give them way.*

Muslims reiterated his graceful lines. The poet in him was saddened when the glorious verse descended saying: *And for the poets, only the erring people follow them* (26:224). But soon he was comforted to hear a subsequent verse saying: *Except those who believe and do deeds of righteousness, and remember God frequently, and defend themselves after being oppressed* (26: 227).

When the Muslims took up arms in self-defence, Ibn Rawahah saw service in all their battles: Badr, Uhud, Khandaq, Al Hudaybiya, and Khaibar. His perpetual slogan was these lines of poetry: "O my soul, death is inevitable, so it is better for you to be martyred." He shouted at the disbelievers in every battle, "O disbelievers get out of my way. My Prophet ﷺ has all the excellent qualities."

The Battle of Mu'tah started, and, as we have mentioned, Abdullah was the third of the commanders, in line after Zaid and Jafar. Ibn Rawahah (may Allah be pleased with him) stood there as the army was about to leave Medina and recited:

> *I truly ask the Most Beneficent's forgiveness*
> *and a mortal stroke of a sword*

that will strike me down
foaming or a mortal stab
with a spear by a stubborn disbeliever
that will make my liver and intestine
show out of my body. So that
when people pass by my grave,
they will say: By Allah, you are
the most righteous warrior.

Indeed, a stroke or a stab that would convey him into the world of rewarded martyrs was his utmost wish. The army marched towards Mu'tah. When the Muslims saw their enemies, they estimated them at 200,000, for they saw endless waves of warriors. The Muslims glanced back at their small group and were stunned. Some of them suggested, "Let us send a message to the Prophet ﷺ to tell him of the enormity of the enemy that surpassed all our expectations so he will either order us to wait for reinforcements or to pierce through the enemy lines."

However, Ibn Rawahah stood amidst the lines of the army and said: "O my people, by Allah, we do not fight our enemies with numbers, strength or equipment, but rather with this religion which Allah has honoured us with. So, go right ahead: it is either one of two equally good options, victory or martyrdom." The Muslims, who were lesser in number and greater in faith, cried out, "By Allah, you spoke the truth." The smaller army broke through the mighty host of 200,000 warriors to face terrible and gruelling battle.

As we have mentioned, both armies met in fierce combat. The first commander, Zaid ibn Haritha, was struck down, gaining a glorious martyrdom thereby. The second in command was Jafar ibn Abu Talib, who felt blessed to be martyred. Abdullah took over the command and grabbed the standard from Jafar's failing upper arms. The battle reached peak ferocity. The smaller army was indistinct amidst the waves of the mighty hosts of Heraclius.

When Ibn Rawahah was a soldier, he attacked confidently. But now the command placed greater responsibilities on his shoulders for the army's safety. It seemed that for a moment he was overtaken by hesitation and dread, yet he instantly shook off those apprehensions, summoned his innate fearlessness and cried out, "O my soul, you look as if you were afraid to cross the way that leads to Paradise. O my soul, I took an oath to fight. O my soul, death is inevitable, so you had better be martyred. Now I will experience the inevitability of death. What you have cared for so long is finally yours. So, go ahead, for if you follow these two heroes, you will be guided to the way of Paradise." He of course meant the two heroes who had preceded him in martyrdom, Zaid and Jafar.

He darted into the Roman armies, fiercely and ruthlessly. Were it not for a previous ordainment from Allah that he was to be martyred on that day, he would have annihilated the fighting hosts. But destiny called to him, and he too was martyred. His body was struck down, yet his pure, valiant spirit was raised to the heavens. His most precious wish finally came true, so that "When people pass by my grave, they will say: By Allah you are the most righteous warrior."

The fierce attack in Al-Balqa in Syria went on. Back in Medina the Prophet ﷺ was talking peacefully and contentedly with his Companions when he suddenly stopped talking. He closed his eyes a little, then opened them. Tinged with sadness and compassion, he looked around him and said, "Zaid took the standard and fought until he was martyred." He was silent for a while, then continued "Jafar grasped it and fought until he was martyred. Then Abdullah ibn Rawahah grasped it and fought until he was martyred." He was silent for a while, then his eyes sparkled with elation, tranquillity, and joy as he said, "They were all raised to Paradise."

What a glorious journey it must have been. They marched together to conquer, and together they were raised up to the heavens. The best salute to immortalise their memory rests in the Prophet's words: "They were raised up to await me in Paradise."

(22)

KHALID IBN AL-WALID

The Sword of Allah

Khalid ibn Al-Walid's story is rather unusual. He was once the deadly enemy of the Muslims at the Battle of Uhud. But, he later became the sworn enemy of *Islam's* enemies in the remaining battles.

Where to begin? Khalid himself only truly felt his life began on the day he met the Prophet ﷺ and pledged allegiance to him. If he could have ruled out all the years that preceded that day, he would not have thought twice.

Let us begin then with the part of his life which he himself loved most. Let us begin from that glorious moment when his heart was affected by Allah, and his spirit was blessed by the Most Merciful. It overflowed with devotion to His religion, His Prophet, and finally ended with a memorable martyrdom in the pursuit of truth. A martyrdom that enabled him to erase the burdens of his falsehood in the past.

One day, Khalid sat alone in deep thought concerning the new religion that was gaining momentum every day. He wished that Allah, the All-Knower of what is hidden and unseen, would guide him to the right path. His blessed heart was revived by the glad tidings of certainty. Therefore, he said to himself, "By Allah, it is crystal clear now. This man is indeed a Prophet, so how long shall I procrastinate? By Allah, I will go and submit myself to Islam." Now, let us hear Khalid (may Allah be pleased with him) narrate his own blessed visit to the Prophet ﷺ, and his journey from Makkah to Medina to join the ranks of the believers:

"*I hoped to find an escort, and I ran into Uthman ibn Talha. When I told him about my intention, he agreed to escort me. We travelled shortly before daybreak and as we reached the plain, we ran into Amr ibn Al-As. After we had exchanged greetings, he asked us about our destination, and when we told him, it turned out that he himself was going to the same place to submit himself to Islam.*

The three of us arrived at Medina on the first day of Safar in the eighth year. As soon as I laid my eyes on the Prophet, I said, "Peace be upon the Prophet," so he greeted me with a bright face. Immediately, I submitted myself to Islam and bore witness to the truth. Finally, the Prophet ﷺ said, "I knew that you have an open mind and I prayed that it would lead you to safety."

I took my oath of allegiance to the Prophet then asked him, "Please ask Allah's forgiveness for me for all the wrongdoings I have committed to hinder men from the path of Allah." The Prophet said, "Islam erases all the wrongdoings committed before it." Yet I pleaded with him, "Please pray for me." Finally, he supplicated Allah, "O Allah, forgive Khalid for all the wrongdoings he committed before he embraced Islam." Then Amr ibn Al-As and Uthman ibn Talha stepped forward and submitted themselves to Islam and gave their oath of allegiance to the Prophet."

Notice his words: "Please ask Allah's forgiveness for me for all the wrongdoings I have committed in the past to hinder men from the path of Allah." When we come across various incidents in the course of Khalid's life story, these words are our key to our understanding of him. For the time being though, let us accompany Khalid (formerly the Quraysh's great leader and warrior) as he turns his back on the idols of his ancestors, and faces the advent of a new world under the standard of Islam.

To start with, let us recall the story of the three martyrs of the Battle of Mu'tah: Zaid ibn Haritha, Jafar ibn Abu Talib and Abdullah ibn Rawahah. They were the heroes of this Battle, where (despite the Romans mobilising 200,000 warriors) the Muslims achieved an unprecedented victory.

Do you recall the words with which the Prophet ﷺ announced the sad news of the death of the three commanders of the battle? "Zaid ibn Haritha took the standard and fought holding it until he died as a martyr; then Jafar took it and fought clinging to it until he won martyrdom; and finally, Abdullah ibn Rawahah grabbed it and held it fast until he won martyrdom." The Prophet's narration of events then went on as follows: "Then it was gripped by a sword of the swords of Allah, and he fought until he achieved victory."

Who was that heroic 'sword of the swords of Allah'? He was none other than Khalid ibn Al-Walid, who threw himself into the battlefield, as if he were an ordinary soldier. After the last commander, Abdullah, had achieved martyrdom, Thabut ibn Aqram took the standard with his right hand and raised it high amidst the Muslim army. His purpose was to stop any potential disarray inside the lines. Thabut then carried the standard and hastened towards Khalid ibn Al-Walid and said, "Take the standard, Abu Sulaiman." Khalid thought that he did not deserve to take it, since he had only recently embraced Islam. He felt he had no right to preside over an army that included the Ansar and Muhajirun, both of whom had preceded him in embracing Islam.

These qualities of decorum, modesty, and gratitude were becoming of Khalid's worthiness. He said, "I will not dare to hold it. Go on, hold it, for you deserve it better than me. First, you are older. Second, you witnessed the Battle of Bad." Thabut answered, "Come on, take it, you know the art of fighting far better than me. By Allah, I only held it to give it to you." Then he called on the Muslims, "Do you vote for Khalid's command?" They readily answered, "Yes we do!"

At that moment, the great warrior mounted his horse and thrust the standard forward with his right hand. It was as if he were knocking on closed doors whose time had finally come to be flung wide open. From that day onwards, Khalid's prosperous career in military leadership took flight.

Although Khalid was in charge of the army command, no military expertise could have changed the course of the battle at that stage. Instead, he focused on damage limitation for the Muslim army, in order to prevent more casualties. Sometimes a great commander must resort to that kind of measure in order to prevent the annihilation of an entire army.

Without hesitation, Khalid flung himself into the vast battlefield. His eyes were as sharp as a hawk's. His mind worked quickly, turning over all the probabilities in his mind. While the battle raged, Khalid quickly split his army into groups, each with an assigned task. He used his incredible expertise and outstanding cunning to create an opening in the Roman army, through which the whole Muslim army retreated intact. This narrow escape was credited to the ingenuity of a Muslim hero. It was after this battle that the Prophet ﷺ gave Khalid the great epithet 'The Sword of Allah'.

Shortly thereafter, the Quraysh violated their treaty with the Prophet ﷺ and the Muslims marched under Khalid's command to conquer Makkah. The Prophet assigned the command of the right flank of the army to Khalid ibn Al-Walid. And so, Khalid re-entered Makkah as one of the commanders of the Muslim army. He recalled his youth when he had galloped across Makkah's plains as commander of the pagan army. Some of these memories weighed heavily on him, and he was still filled with remorse for his wasted time.

But as Makkah shook with the victory cry, "There is no god but Allah", and "Allahu akbar", Khalid raised his head in satisfaction at seeing the standard of Islam fluttering on the Makkan horizon. He said to himself, *"Indeed, it is a promise of Allah and Allah fails not in His promise."* (Quran 30:6) Then, Khalid bent his head in gratitude to Allah for all the guidance that led him to this moment.

Khalid was always near the Prophet ﷺ. He devoted his excellent abilities to the service of a religion he firmly believed in, and to which he devoted his life. After the beloved Prophet died and Abu Bakr became Caliph, a group of sly apostates from Islam emerged in an attempt to stifle the new religion. Abu Bakr immediately chose the Sword of Allah, Khalid ibn Al-Walid, to steer them against these people. Although Abu Bakr himself was at the head of the first wave, he let Khalid mastermind and orchestrate the final decisive battle - largely considered the most dangerous of all the apostasy battles.

As the apostate armies were taking measures to perfect their conspiracy, the great Caliph Abu Bakr insisted on heading up the Muslim army. The Companions tried desperately to persuade him not to, but his mind was made up. Perhaps he meant to give the cause for battle a special importance. He could not achieve this except by his actual participation in battle, and his direct command of some or all of the Muslim troops.

In spite of the fact that it started as an accidental insubordination, the outbreak of apostasy posed a serious threat. Soon, the opportunistic enemies of Islam - whether from the Arab tribes or from across the borders in Rome and Persia - seized their last chance to ebb the tide of Islam. They instigated mutiny and chaos from afar.

Unfortunately, such mutiny flowed like an electric current through the Arab tribes, such as Asad, Ghatfan, Abs, Tii, Dhubyan; then on to Banu Amar, Hawazin, Sulaim and Banu Tamim. The skirmishes had hardly begun with a few soldiers, when they were reinforced with enormous armies, often of thousands of warriors. The people of Bahrain, Oman and Al-Mahrah all responded to this divisive plot.

Suddenly, Islam was in a dangerous predicament, and the apostate enemy closed in upon the believers. But, Abu Bakr was ready for them. He mobilised the Muslim armies and marched to where the armies of Banu Abs, Banu Murah and Banu Dhubyan had gathered. The battle went on for quite some time before the Muslims achieved their victory. But, no sooner had the victorious Muslim army reached Medina, than the Caliph was forced to send it on another expedition. News spread that the armies of the apostates were increasing in number and weapons by the hour.

And so, Abu Bakr began marching at the head of a second wave, only this time the prominent Companions lost their patience and insisted that the Caliph should remain in Medina. Accordingly, Imam Ali stood in Abu Bakr's way as he marched out, and held the reins of his she-camel asking, "Where to, Caliph of the Prophet? I will tell you the same words that the Prophet told you in the Battle of Uhud: Sheathe your sword, Abu Bakr, and don't expose us to such a tragic loss at this critical time."

The Caliph was forced to comply with the consensus. Therefore, he split the army into 11 divisions and assigned a certain role for each one. Khalid ibn Al-Walid was to be the commander over a large division. When the Caliph gave every commander his standard, he addressed Khalid saying, "I heard the Prophet say, 'Khalid is truly an excellent slave of Allah and a brother of the same tribe. He is a sword of Allah unsheathed against disbelievers and hypocrites'."

Khalid and his army fought one battle after another and achieved one victory after another until they reached the final, crucial battle. It was in the Battle of Yamama that Banu Hanifah, and their allies from other Arab tribes, organised one of the most dangerous armies of the apostasy, led by Musailamah the Liar. A number of Muslim forces tried to defeat Musailamah's army but failed. Finally, the Caliph ordered Khalid to march to where Banu Hanifah was camped.

No sooner had Musailamah heard that Khalid was on his way to fight him than he reorganised his army, forming a devastating enemy. Both armies met in fierce combat. Khalid's army stopped at a sand dune that overlooked Yamama. At the same time, Musailamah marched with great might, followed by endless waves of soldiers. Khalid assigned the brigades and standard to the commanders of his army. As the two armies clashed in a terrible war, the Muslim martyrs fell one by one. Immediately Khalid realised that the enemy was about to win the battle, so he galloped up a nearby hill and surveyed the battlefield. He realised that his soldiers morale was waning under the pressure of the blitz of Musailamah's army.

He decided to reinvigorate his soldiers, so he summoned the flanks and reorganised their positions on the battlefield. He cried out victoriously, "Fight together in your own groups and let us see who will surpass the other and win the field." They all obeyed and reorganised themselves in their own groups. Thus, the Muhajirun fought under their standard, the Ansar fought under theirs, and every group fought under its standard. As a result, the Muslims were charged with admirable enthusiasm and determination.

Every now and then, Khalid was careful to cry out, "Allahu akbar" and "There is no god but Allah." He ordered his army in such a way that he turned the swords of his men into an inevitable victory. Strikingly, in a short space of time, the Muslim army turned the tables on Musailamah's army. The enemy's soldiers fell like flies in tens, then hundreds, then thousands. Khalid commanded his soldiers with an electric enthusiasm. In the end, Musailamah was slain and the bodies of his army were scattered on the battlefield. Finally, the standard of the imposter was buried forever.

On hearing the good news, the Caliph offered the *salat al-shukr* (prayer of thanks) to Allah for bestowing victory on the hands of the heroic Khalid. Abu Bakr had enough insight to realise the danger of the powers perched on their borders, threatening the future of Islam. His main concerns were the Persians in Iraq and the Romans in Syria. These two dwindling empires clung tenaciously to the distorted remnants of their past glories. And they were not only afflicting the people of Iraq and Syria with horrible torments, but also manipulating their opinion. The majority of their population were Arab, but they had still instigated them to fight the Muslim Arabs. Therefore, the Caliph sent his next orders to Khalid to march towards Iraq. Upon his arrival, the first thing that Khalid did was to dispatch messages to every governor and deputy who ruled the provinces of Iraq. These messages read as follows:

"*In the name of Allah, the Most Beneficent, the Most Merciful. Khalid ibn Al-Walid sends this message to the satraps of Persia. Peace will be upon him who follows the guidance. All praises and thanks be to Allah Who dispersed your power and thwarted your deceitful plots. On the one hand, he who performs our prayers directing his face to our Qibla to face the Sacred Mosque in Makkah and eats our slaughtered animals is a Muslim. He has the same rights and duties that we have. On the other hand, if you do not want to embrace Islam, then as soon as you receive my message, send over the jizya (tax levied upon non-Muslim people who are under the protection of a Muslim government) and I give you my word that I will respect and honour this covenant. But if you do not agree to either choice, then, by Allah, I will send to you people who rave death as much as you crave life.*"

Khalid had planted scouts everywhere, and they warned him against the enormity of the armies in Iraq. As usual, Khalid did not waste much time. Therefore, he flung his soldiers against the disbelievers, to devastate their plans.

Victory followed him wherever he went, from Al-Ubullah, to As-Sadir, An-Najaf, Al-Hirah, Al-Anbar then Al-Kadhimiyah. The glad tidings of Khalid's arrival blew like a fresh breeze wherever he went to spread Islam. The weak and oppressed found sanctuary in the new religion that saved them from the occupation and oppression of the Persians. Khalid's first order to his troops was always, "Do not attack or hurt the peasants. Leave them to work at peace unless some of them attack you. Only then, do I permit you to defend yourselves." And so, he marched on with his victorious army, swept his enemies aside, and cut through their ranks. The adhan rang out everywhere.

Even the thought of the Islamic call to prayer cast fear into the Roman occupation in Syria. So, in a desperate attempt to recapture the phantom of their empire, they hurriedly prepared for battle.

Abu Bakr Al-Siddiq mobilised his armies and chose a group of his prominent commanders to lead them. This included Abu Ubaidah ibn Al-Jarrah, Amr ibn Al-As, Yazid ibn Abu Sufyan and Muawiyah ibn Abu Sufyan. When the Roman emperor heard of the mobilisation of these armies, he advised his ministers to make peace with the Muslims to avoid an inevitable defeat. However, his advisers insisted on fighting and maintained, "By our Lord, we will make Abu Bakr's hair stand on end before his horses breed in our land." Consequently, they mobilised an army estimated at 240,000 warriors.

The Muslim commanders dispatched this terrifying news to Abu Bakr, who pledged, "By Allah, I will rid them of their doubts through Khalid." Thus, the antidote to the Roman whisperings of mutiny and disbelief was Khalid ibn Al-Walid himself. Khalid promptly acted upon his orders and left Iraq under Al-Muthanna ibn Haritha's supervision and marched with his troops until they reached the Muslim headquarters in Syria. His ingenuity enabled him to organise the Muslim armies and coordinate their different positions in no time. Shortly before the outbreak of war, he addressed his warriors after he had praised and thanked Allah, saying, "This is Allah's day. On this day, we must not give way to pride not let injustice overrule. I advise you to purify your jihad and your deeds for Allah. Let us take turns in command. Let each and every one of us take over the command for a day."

Khalid inspired his troops with this motivational speech. Rather than endorsing arrogance, he reiterated that it was "Allah's day" and that "we must not give way to pride nor let injustice overrule." In spite of the fact that the Caliph himself had assigned the command of the army to Khalid, he did not want to give Satan a chance to whisper into the breasts of his soldiers. Therefore, he relinquished his absolute hold on the army to every soldier in the ranks, by rotating the commander from day to day.

The enormous and well-equipped Roman army was truly terrifying. However, the Roman commander realised that time was in the Muslims' favour, and they were often inclined towards protracted battles to achieve their victory. Therefore, he decided to mobilise all their troops to aim for a quick battle and finish off the Arabs, once and for all.

Undoubtedly the courageous Muslims, on that day, were gripped by fear and anxiety. Yet, in such predicaments they always resorted to their faith, where they found hope and victory. Notwithstanding the might of the Roman armies, the experienced Abu Bakr had firm belief in Khalid's abilities. Therefore, he said, "Khalid is the man for it. By Allah, I will rid them of their doubts with Khalid."

Ibn Al-Walid rallied his army, then divided it into brigades. He laid out a new plan for attack and defence that adhered to the Roman tactics of war - strategies with which he was well-acquainted from his past experience with the Persians. He was ready for all possibilities. Strangely enough, the battle played out exactly as he had imagined it would.

Khalid believed that the ingenuity of victory and firmness were one and the same. Before the two armies clashed, he was worried about the possibility that some of the soldiers, especially those who had newly embraced Islam, might flee upon seeing the terrifying and enormous Roman army. It was his view that the Muslim army could not afford the loss of even one of its soldiers, for it was enough to spread malignant panic inside the army - something that even the entire Roman army could not succeed in doing. Consequently, he was very firm concerning anyone who deserted his post and weapon and ran away. In the Battle of Yarmuk in particular, he summoned the Muslim women and, for the first time, gave them swords. He ordered them to stand at the rear of the lines to: "Kill anyone who flees." It was a touch of mastermind.

Shortly before the battle erupted, the Roman commander asked Khalid to show himself, for he wanted a few words with him. Khalid rode towards him, then they galloped to the area that separated the two armies. Mahan, the Roman commander, addressed Khalid saying, "We know that nothing but weariness and hunger made you leave your country and go on this expedition. If you wish, we shall give ten dinars, clothes, and food to every one of you, on one condition, that you return to your country and next year we will do the same."

Khalid gnashed his teeth, as he was provoked by his flagrant lack of manners, yet he repressed himself and answered confidently, "We didn't leave our country out of hunger as you said, but we heard that Roman blood is delicious, so we have decided to quench our thirst with it." Swiftly, the hero rode back to the ranks of his army and raised the Muslim standard to the full length of his arm, then he launched the attack.

At once, his army charged like a missile into the battlefield. They clashed in extraordinary and deadly combat. The Romans rushed in with their great numbers, only to find that their foes were not easy prey. The self-sacrifice and firmness that the Muslims displayed on that day was beyond impressive.

In the first instance, one of the Muslim soldiers rushed to Abu Ubaidah ibn Al-Jarrah (may Allah be pleased with him) during the battle and said, "I have set my mind on martyrdom. Do you want me to take a message to the Prophet ﷺ when I meet him?" Abu Ubaidah answered, "Yes, tell him we have indeed found true what our Lord had promised us." Immediately, the man darted like an arrow into the battlefield. He fought fiercely with his one sword, as thousands of swords were thrusted towards him, until finally he achieved his martyrdom.

Secondly, Ikramah ibn Abu Jahl (the son of the infamous Abu Jahl) called out to the Muslims when the Romans were killing anyone who came within the range of their swords and said: "I fought against the Prophet before Allah guided me to Islam, so how can I possibly be afraid of fighting Allah's enemy after I submitted myself to Islam?" Then he cried out, "Who gives me the pledge to death?" He was given the pledge to death by a group of Muslims, and then they all broke through the enemy lines. They preferred martyrdom to victory. Allah accepted the bargain through their pledge, and they won their martyrdom.

Thirdly, other Muslims were badly wounded and so water was brought to quench their thirst. But, when it was offered to the first of the wounded, he pointed to his brother who was lying next to him more seriously wounded and who was more thirsty. Again, when this brother was offered water, he in his turn pointed to his brother. So many of them died thirsty in just demonstrating this incredible act of self-sacrifice. In this and many other ways, the Battle of Yarmuk witnessed unprecedented examples of sacrifice.

Among these striking images of the battle, we also find the extraordinary portrait of Khalid ibn Al-Walid. At the head of (according to some reports) only 100 soldiers who threw themselves against 40,000 Romans, Khalid kept calling out: "By Allah, the Romans seemed to have lost their patience and courage, therefore I pray to Allah to let you have the upper hand over them."

How could as few as 100 soldiers have the upper hand over 40,000? It seems implausible, but we must remember the hearts of these soldiers were filled with faith in Allah, the Most High, the Most Great.

Filled with faith in His trustworthy and honest Prophet ﷺ. And, was not their Caliph Abu Bakr Al-Siddiq - the man who raised Islam's flag throughout the world, but would still milk ewes for widows and knead bread for orphans? Was not their Commander Khalid ibn Al-Walid - the antidote for tyranny, arrogance and transgression? So, the breeze of victory blew over those soldiers, mighty and victorious.

———•◊•———

Khalid's ingenuity impressed the Roman officers and commanders so much so that Jerjah, a Roman commander, asked Khalid to show himself during a rest in the fighting. When they met, the Roman commander asked him, "Khalid, tell me the truth and do not lie, for the freeman doesn't lie. Did Allah send down on your Prophet a heavenly sword and he gave it to you, so that it enables you to kill anyone who comes within its sweep?" Khalid answered, "No." The man exclaimed, "Then why do they call you the 'Sword of Allah'?" Khalid explained, "Allah sent His Prophet to us. Some of us believed in him and others disbelieved in him. I was among the disbelievers until Allah guided my heart to Islam and to His Prophet ﷺ and I gave him my allegiance. Therefore, the Prophet supplicated Allah for me and said, 'You are the Sword of Allah.'"

The Roman commander went on to ask, "What do you invite people to?" Khalid answered, "We invite people to monotheism and to Islam." He asked, "Does anyone who submits himself to Islam have the same reward as you?" Khalid answered, "Yes, and even better." Jerjah exclaimed, "How, when you embraced Islam before he did?" Khalid answered, "We lived with the Prophet and saw with our own eyes his signs and miracles. Now anyone who had the chance to see what we saw and hear what we heard was expected to submit himself to Islam sooner or later. As for you who did not see or hear him, if despite this you believe in him and in the Unseen, you will find better and greater reward if you purify your conscience and intentions to Allah." The Roman commander cried out as he urged his horse closer to Khalid and stood next to him, "Please, Khalid, teach me Islam!" He submitted himself to Islam and prayed two rakahs. Soon, combat erupted and once again, the Roman Jerjah fought, but this time on the Muslim side until he won martyrdom.

Now, let us watch closely how human greatness was manifested in

Khalid, during one of the battle's most remarkable scenes. One historic narration says that while Khalid was commanding the Muslim army in this crucial war, and wrestling victory out of the claws of the Romans, he received a message from the new Caliph, Umar ibn Al-Khattab. He dispatched a message to Khalid, saluting the Muslim army and announcing the sad news of Abu Bakr's death (may Allah be pleased with him). Then he ordered Khalid to give up his command to Abu Ubaidah ibn Al-Jarrah. Khalid read the message and supplicated Allah to have mercy on Abu Bakr and bestow His guidance on Umar. Then he strictly ordered the messenger not to tell anyone about the purport of the message and not to leave his place or communicate with anyone.

Then Khalid resumed his command of the combat and concealed the news of Abu Bakr's death and Umar's orders until they had achieved victory. Finally, the hour of victory came and the Romans were defeated. It was only then that the hero approached Abu Ubaidah and saluted him. At first, Abu Ubaidah thought that he did so in jest, yet he soon realised how serious and true this news was. Instantly, he kissed Khalid between his eyes and praised his greatness.

The second version of the same incident retells that the message was sent to Abu Ubaidah, who concealed the news from Khalid until the burden of war was over. Which of the two versions is authentic is not our concern. The only thing that interests us here is Khalid's conduct, which was admirable in both accounts.

I cannot think of a situation in which Khalid displayed more loyalty and sincerity than this one. It did not matter to him whether he was a commander or a soldier. Both ranks were one and the same to him, as long as they enabled him to carry out his duties towards Allah and the Prophet ﷺ, to whom he gave allegiance in the name of Islam. This immense self-control from both Khalid and other Muslims at the time would not have been possible without the guidance of the unique Caliphs, Abu Bakr and Umar.

Notwithstanding the fact that Khalid and Umar were not exactly the best of friends, Umar's decency, justice, and remarkable greatness were not in the least questioned by Khalid. Hence, his decisions and judgments were not questioned.

Umar, the Commander of the Faithful, had nothing against Khalid but found his sword overbearing. He vented these reservations when he suggested to Abu Bakr that Khalid should be dismissed after the death of Malik ibn Nuwairah. He said, "Khalid's sword is overburdening." He meant that it was too swift and harsh. The Caliph Al-Siddiq said, "I would not sheathe what Allah had unsheathed against the disbelievers." Notice that Umar did not say that Khalid was overburdening but used "overburdening" to describe the sword, rather than the man. Not only did these words embody Umar's politeness, but also his profound appreciation of Khalid nonetheless.

Khalid was a man of war from head to toe. He dedicated his whole life before and after his Islam to becoming a shrewd and daring knight. Even his environment and the way he was brought up were devoted to that ultimate goal.

Whenever he looked back, all he saw were the wars he waged against the Prophet ﷺ, and the strokes of his sword that had slain believers. Those memories agitated Khalid and made him conscience-stricken. Therefore, his sword longed to devastate the pillars of disbelief to compensate for his wrongdoings in the past.

You will recall Khalid asking the Prophet ﷺ: "Please ask Allah's forgiveness for me for all the wrongdoings I committed to hinder men from Allah's path." You will also remember that even when the Prophet told him that Islam erases all the wrongdoings committed before it, he pleaded with him until he finally promised him to ask Allah's forgiveness for all his mischief prior to Islam.

Imagine, the sword of a warrior such as Khalid being thrust upon the commands of a conscience. Then, that sword is revived by purification and absolute loyalty to a religion. When such a sword is surrounded by animosity and conspiracy against that new religion, surely it would be impossible for that sword to throw aside its strict principles?

For instance, when the Prophet ﷺ sent Khalid to some Arab tribes after the conquest of Makkah, he said to him, "I am sending you there not as a warrior, but as a Muslim who invites to the way of Allah." Sadly, his sword got the better of him and he did indeed turn warrior during a particularly lethal encounter. Khalid thereby nullified his role as a Muslim envoy, inviting others to the way of Allah as he had been ordered. When the Prophet ﷺ heard what Khalid had done, he was stricken with anxiety. He turned in the direction of the Qibla and raised his hands in supplication and apology to Allah, and said, "O Allah, I free myself from blame for what Khalid has committed." Then he sent Ali to give compensatory blood-money to the family of the deceased.

Narrators said that Khalid absolved himself from blame when he clarified that Abdullah ibn Hudhafah As-Sahmi told him: "The Prophet has ordered you to attack them for their rejection of Islam." Regardless, Khalid had always possessed superhuman energy. If we watched him pulling down the statue of Uzza, an idol that the Prophet ﷺ ordered him to destroy, we would see the violent resentment he showed when doing so. He was so aggressive that he did not seem to be striking at a mass of rock but at a whole army. For he kept striking with his right hand, then with his left hand, then with his foot. He yelled at the scattered rubble and dust, "Uzza, I don't believe in you! Glory is not to be yours! I can see that Allah has humiliated you!"

─────·◊·─────

We would do well to repeat Umar's words about Khalid: "Women who give birth to men like Khalid are extremely rare," as well as Umar's earnest wish that Khalid's sword would lose its brashness. On the day of his death though, Umar cried excessively. Later, people learned that his grief was not only caused by his personal loss, but also by the loss of his last chance to return the command to Khalid.

The hero Khalid had rushed to take his place in Paradise. For it was about time he caught his breath, so that his exhausted body could sleep for a while. His restless nature was well known, and he was described by both friends and enemies alike as, "A sleepless man who would not let anyone sleep."

If it were his choice, he would have lived on to demolish all the decaying ruins of the ancient world, and continue his jihad in the way of Allah and Islam. The sweet fragrance of this man's spirit, however, lingers on. We feel his presence whenever swords shimmer and standards flutter over Muslim armies. These were his finest moments. He himself used to say, "Nothing is dearer to me than a frosty night in the company of an infantry of Muhajirun when we are to attack the disbelievers in the morning. Not even the night in which I was wedded to a new bride or received the glad tidings of the birth of a new child."

Therefore, the tragedy of his life, in his opinion, was dying in his bed, after spending an entire lifetime on horseback, sword in hand. It was difficult for him to accept such a death, after all the battles he had fought next to the Prophet ﷺ. All this, after he annihilated the Roman and Persian empires, then galloped to Iraq and Syria where he achieved one victory after another.

In spite of his military station, he was so modest that if you saw him, you would not have distinguished him from his own soldiers. Yet, at the same time, you would have known at once that he was a commander from the way he shouldered responsibilities and put himself forth as a good example. But, again, the tragedy of this hero's life was dying in bed. He said as his tears flowed, "All the battles I fought in left my body scarred with wounds and stabs everywhere, yet here I am dying in bed as if I had never witnessed war before. I hope that the cowards will not have a day's rest even after I am dead."

These words were becoming of such a man. When his moment of departure was near, he dictated his will. Can you guess to whom he left all his valuables? It was to Umar ibn Al-Khattab himself. Can you guess what were his valuables? They were his horse and his weapon. Nothing else.

Thus, his only obsession while he was alive was achieving victory over the enemies of truth. He was not in the least obsessed with the worldly life, with all its splendours and luxury. There was just one thing that he obsessively cherished and treasured. It was his helmet. He lost it in the Battle of Yarmuk, and he exhausted himself and others in searching for it. When he was criticised for that, he said, "I keep it for luck, for it has some hairs of the Prophet's forehead. It makes me feel optimistic that victory is within reach."

———•◊•———

Finally, the body of the hero left his home, carried on the shoulders of his companions. Khalid's mother took one last look at her son, her eyes full of determination but tinged with sadness. She commended him to Allah's protection and said, "There are far, far better than a thousand men who flung themselves into the battlefield. Do you ask me about his valour? He was much more courageous than an enormous lion that protects its cubs in the time of danger. Do you ask me about his generosity? He was far more generous than an overwhelming torrential rain that slides down from the mountains." Umar's heart throbbed and his eyes flowed with tears when he heard her words, and he replied, "You spoke the truth. By Allah, he was everything you said he was."

The hero was buried. His companions stood at his grave in reverence. It was as if the whole world went into mourning. I imagine that this awesome stillness was broken only by the neighing of a horse, tugging at its halter as it followed its master's scent to his grave. Fixing its eyes on the grave, the horse keeps raising and lowering its head as if bidding its final farewell to its master. Khalid bequeathed his horse and weapons to Umar to act in the service of Allah. But, who was valiant enough to deserve to mount it after Khalid?

Let us now repeat after Umar, with the sweet elegy he used to bid farewell to Khalid: "May Allah have mercy on you, Abu Sulaiman. What you have now is far better than what you had in life, for you are now with Allah. You were honoured in life and content in death."

(23)

QAIS IBN SA'AD IBN UBADAH

The Craftiest of Arabs, but for Islam

Although he was young, the Ansar treated Qais as a leader. They used to say, "If only we could buy him a beard!" But who was this lad, who only lacked in appearance for what he made up for otherwise in greatness and excellent leadership?

This young man was Qais ibn Sa'ad ibn Ubadah. He belonged to one of the most distinguished and generous Arab houses, about which the Prophet ﷺ remarked, "Generosity is the prevailing trait of this family." He was a crafty young man, and there was no end to his cleverness. He spoke the truth when he said, "If it were not for Islam, I would have used my craftiness to outwit all the Arabs."

He was sharp-witted and resourceful. In the As-Siffin Battle, he sided with Ali against Muawiyah. He sat there turning over in his mind the plot that would make Muawiyah and his men the worst losers, but the more he thought about his plot, the more he realised that it came under the category of evil plotting. He then repeated Allah's verse to himself: "*But the evil plot encompasses only him who makes it*" (35:43). Consequently, he rejected the plot altogether and asked Allah's forgiveness, saying, "By Allah, if Muawiyah is destined to have the upper hand over us, he will not have it because he has outwitted us, but because our piety and fear of Allah have run short."

Qais was one of the Ansar, from the Khazraj tribe. He belonged to a great family and inherited all the excellent qualities of his ancestors. He was the son of Sa'ad ibn Ubadah, the Khazraj leader. When his father, Sa'ad, submitted himself to Islam, he held his son Qais' hand and introduced him to the Prophet ﷺ saying, "This is your servant from now on." The Prophet saw in Qais all the qualities of excellence and righteousness, so he asked him to sit next to him and said, "This place will always be filled by him for the rest of his life." Anas, the Companion of Allah's Prophet ﷺ said, "Qais ibn Sa'ad ibn Ubadah was to the Prophet like a chief officer to a commander."

Before his Islam, he was so crafty to the extent that no one was able to get the better of him. The people of Medina and its surroundings fell short of his cunning. When he embraced Islam, it turned his life, and even his disposition, upside down, as it taught him how to treat people with sincerity rather than deceit. He was a truly faithful and loyal Muslim. Therefore, he threw aside his cunning manoeuvres. Yet, whenever he faced a difficult situation, his restrained cunning tried to rebel and gain control over him. The only thing that made him come to grips with it were these repeated words to himself: "If it were not for Islam, I would have used my craftiness to outwit all the Arabs."

His cleverness was surpassed only by his generosity. Generosity was not an accidental behaviour on Qais' part, for he belonged to a family renowned for its generosity. It was the custom in those times for all the wealthy and generous people to bid a crier to stand on a high place in the daytime to call guests and passers-by to come for food and rest. Then, at night, he would light a fire to guide strangers to where food was. People at that time used to say, "He who likes fat and meat must go to Dulim ibn Haritha's house for food." Now, Dulim was Qais' great-grandfather. Thus, Qais was suckled amidst both generosity and charity in this high-born family.

One day, both Abu Bakr and Umar commented on his generosity saying, "If we let this lad give free rein to his generosity, he would exhaust his father's wealth." When Sa'ad ibn Ubadah heard about what they had said, he cried out, "Abu Quhafah and ibn Al-Khattab should not have tried to encourage my son to become a miser!"

One day, he lent a debtor who was experiencing hard times a large sum of money. At the appointed time for repayment, this man went to repay his debt to Qais, yet he refused saying, "I never take back anything that I have given."

Human nature is unchangeable. Both generosity and courage are inseparable. Indeed, genuine generosity and courage are like twins: neither is found on its own. If you meet a generous man who is not courageous, then be certain that what you have seen is not real generosity, but a mere pretence. On the other hand, if you find someone who is courageous but not generous, then be certain that what you have seen is not courage, but merely a reckless whim. Qais ibn Sa'ad held the reins of generosity with his right hand, along with courage in his left. It seems as if he was meant for these lines of poetry:

If a flag was hoisted in celebration of glory

Then it must have been held by the right hand of an Arab.

His valour was outstanding in all the battles in which he fought, both during the Prophet's ﷺ life and after his death. When courage depends on honesty and confrontation (rather than prevarication or manipulation), then there is often trouble for that individual. Ever since Qais threw aside his incredible skill of cunning and held onto his straightforward courage, he felt relieved and content - notwithstanding the problems he had to confront as a result of it.

Genuine courage stems solely out of conviction. This conviction is not affected by desire or whim, but rather by truthfulness and honesty with one's self. Hence, when the conflict between Ali and Muawiyah started, Qais tried to side with the one whom he believed to be in the right. Once he decided that Ali was right, he did not hesitate to support him with pride.

Qais was one of the fearless heroes of As-Siffin, Al-Jamal and An-Nahrawan. He carried the Ansar's standard and cried out, "The standard that I'm carrying now is the same one that I used to carry when we marched for war with the Prophet ﷺ and had Jibril as our reinforcement. Any man who has no one but the Ansar on his side is a lucky man."

So, Imam Ali assigned the brave Qais to govern Egypt. At that time, Muawiyah had his sights set on Egypt. He considered it the most precious jewel in his prospective crown. Therefore, no sooner had Muawiyah heard that Qais was to govern Egypt, than he lost his self-control. He became convinced that Qais would stand in his way of ruling Egypt, even if he achieved a decisive victory over Imam Ali. Hence, he used all his cunning methods and unscrupulous tricks to defame Qais before Ali.

Finally, Imam Ali ordered him to leave Egypt. Qais had a legitimate chance to use his cleverness, for he realised that Muawiyah must have incited Ali against him, by casting doubts on Qais' loyalty to him. Therefore, the best answer to Muawiyah's plot was to show more loyalty to Ali to prove Muawiyah wrong. This loyalty was not a mere pretence on Qais' part, but rather his firm conviction. He did not feel for a moment that he was unfairly dismissed from his position, as Qais only considered the governorship as a means to an end, namely, to serve his faith and religion. He dedicated himself to the service of the truth. Whether he maintained his governorship of Egypt or stood by Imam Ali in the battlefield, it was one and the same thing for him, as long as they were a means to attain truth.

When Muawiyah left the Muslims no other way out but to unsheathe their swords against one another, Qais took the command of 5,000 Muslims who shared in the mourning for Imam Ali's death. Hasan thought that it would be best to put an end to the prolonged suffering of Muslims and that deadly conflict.

Therefore, he agreed to negotiate with Muawiyah and finally gave him his oath of allegiance. When this happened, Qais pondered the matter in his mind and decided that no matter how right Hasan was in his decision, his soldiers had every right to be consulted. Thus, he called them together and addressed them saying, "If you wish, we will keep on fighting to the last breath, or if you wish, I will ask Muawiyah to guarantee your safety and security." They opted for the latter, and Muawiyah was truly relieved to be rid of one of his most dreaded foes.

This man, whose craftiness was tamed and subdued by Islam, died in 59 AH in Medina. Qais ibn Sa'ad ibn Ubadah, the man who used to say, "If I did not hear the Prophet say, 'Craftiness and deceit reside in hell,' I would have been the craftiest man of the nation."

FAREWELL

While we bid farewell to the graceful company of the Companions of the Prophet Muhammad (may peace and blessings be upon him and upon them all), we may ask ourselves, have we taken into account all of those great men? The answer is, quite simply, no. We have been honoured to closely examine a blessed number of them, but we were not fortunate enough to accompany all the Companions.

Indeed, the 60 men introduced in this book represent many thousands of others who saw the Messenger ﷺ, lived during his time, believed in him, and struggled with him. In the lives of these 60 righteous men though, we perceive an image of all the Companions. We see their faith, their steadfastness, their heroism, their sacrifices, and their loyalty. I desire not to repeat what I have already written about the amazing faith which filled the hearts of these men. But, we recognise all of their efforts and the victories they achieved in the name of Islam.

These 60 men then, are a superb example to us all. These heroes lived through a great age of human struggle and of especial religious struggle. It was an age when the ancient world was overtaken by a new force of truth. A truth which came to announce the oneness of Allah and the unity of His creation. There were no idols in this new era, no deified emperors or czars. It recognised that there is only One God Who is Allah, and all His people are as equal in His eyes as the teeth of a comb.

———•◊•———

Muhammad ﷺ with his truth, steadfastness, purity, and eminence could not but reflect a rare quality of faith on the people around him. It was the faith of people who had known him well and had seen him in all his grace. They saw his humanity and his devotion to Allah; his loftiness and modesty; his superb qualities and his simplicity; his strength and his compassion.

They observed him, understood his noble motives, and mimicked his undeviating methods. Therefore, no doubt could prevent them from believing in him. Every nation has asked its prophet for a miracle in order to believe in him, all except Muhammad's Companions, the men around the Prophet ﷺ. They never said, "Show us a miracle as proof of your truthfulness." This was because Muhammad himself was the miracle. Seeking another miracle outside of him, his personality, and his principles would have been a kind of naivety. Their hearts had instead been filled with the guidance of Allah, and their perceptions had been illuminated with His light.

The faith of that first generation of Muslims instigated a revival of humanity, with its different religions, different ages and races. Before Islam, they were merely scattered, discordant tribes led by inflexible narrow-minded individuality. As a political power, they had not achieved anything of note. And, as an economic power, they were the poorest of people.

So, how did these minorities become the architects of a new world? Was it the power of weapons and the plenitude of armies? Surely not. Alexander before them and Genghis Khan after them had plenty of weapons and soldiers. Where is Alexander today? Where is Genghis Khan? What is left of them and their astounding victories? What is left of all that, in the conscience of mankind? Nothing.

Therefore, materialistic power was not the reason that turned the Companions of the Messenger ﷺ into what we have seen here. It was only faith; faith in the truth and in what is good. Above that, faith in the Lord of truth and good. This is the true lesson taught by Muhammad, the Messenger of Allah (may Allah be pleased with him and his Companions).

When people devote their lives to benefaction, surely darkness turns into light, chaos into order, and weakness into strength. In this pursuit of truth, property becomes protected, humiliation becomes greatness, privation becomes plenitude, and ignorance becomes knowledge. That was what the Messenger ﷺ and his Companions did, just as the messengers and their companions before them. And it is the lesson they left us to learn from.

Truth and benefaction were the essence of the role of the Messenger and his Companions. A pure and brave faith was their core principle. Because of those values, they bequeathed the best inheritance to humanity. They filled the human conscience with a sense of integrity.

Today, most radio stations worldwide openly broadcast verses from the glorious Quran. The Quran was a guide and a light to the Messenger ﷺ and his Companions. Now, all over the earth, in communities of Muslims, Christians, Jews, Hindus, Buddhists, atheists and so on - lofty minarets are erected to repeat the same words of the Messenger's muezzin 1400 years ago...

> *Allah is the Greatest, Allah is the Greatest*
> *I bear witness that there is no god but Allah*
> *I bear witness that Muhammad is the Messenger of Allah*
> *Come to the Prayer*
> *Come to success*

The Quran is recited the world over; everywhere on earth the mosques are filled; and everywhere on earth its principles are celebrated. This all-pervading power comes only from belief in Allah, in the Messenger, and in all other messengers who came before. They truly gave everything to their cause and took nothing for themselves.

There remains one question raised by this study of the Prophet's Companions. The question is, "How could dispute have ruined the strong ties between the rightly guided brothers? And, how did the civil war (that broke out between Ali's supporters and those of Muawiyah) overpower this splendid brotherhood?"

In order to give an answer to this question, we have to go back to the virtue of faith in these Companions, and consider other historical factors as well. Indeed, their true, clear, and decisive faith had made them follow the same path. To them, truth had but one face which they recognised and followed. While the Messenger ﷺ was living among them, guidance to what is true and right - a matter in which people differed - was an easy matter. Revelation, or the Messenger (or a combination both), usually clarified every obscure or unintelligible matter.

When the Messenger ﷺ passed away, they never differed in what had been explained by Allah's revelation or through Muhammad's interpretation. However, when Uthman (may Allah be pleased with him) was killed, his murder was preceded and accompanied by a pernicious commotion that shook all Islamic nations at that time. As a consequence of that terrible occurrence, the dispute widened. It was inevitable for each Companion to choose to adopt one of the multiple views, according to his own demeanour.

Their way of choosing, like their way of believing, was characterised by clarity and decisiveness. There was no hesitation or hypocrisy. Those who were convinced of Imam Ali's point of view chose his side, and those convinced of Muawiyah's point of view chose his side. Some chose to be neutral and abandoned the dispute altogether.

The above concerns the Companions, the early believers in Islam who lived at the time of the Messenger ﷺ and fought with him the forces of polytheism and darkness. However, these Companions alone were not the 'centre of gravity' in the Islamic state at the time of the dispute between Ali and Muawiyah. This is because the state at that time had expanded tremendously, and a new power emerged and started to take part in and direct events. The best evidence for this is that the conspiracy to claim the life of Caliph Uthman and the agents assigned to carry it out came from outside Medina, rather from outside the Arab Peninsula. They came from some distant Islamic countries. Therefore, this new foreign power played a role which the first Companions struggled to repel.

This new power was effective in turning the dispute between Ali and Muawiyah into outright warfare. It was only then that the people of Syria sided with Muawiyah, and the people of Iraq sided with Ali, making them the real protagonists in that war. Even in the final analysis, the war was not between two Islamic camps as much as it was between two regional ones: the Syrians on one side and Iraqis on the other.

There was a third force which cannot be ignored, a force which lay in wait for Islam since it had its sovereignty demolished. That was the remnants of power in Persia and some few who continued to perpetuate their schemes against Islam through their many agents who infiltrated Islam by pretending to embrace it. Some of them were able to cause a lot of damage and destruction within the ranks of Muslims, which the defeated empires could not otherwise do alone.

We should also not ignore another fact, which is that each of the leaders never expected that the matter would develop to such a terrible degree. Imam Ali and his followers saw their advance towards Syria as merely a scare tactic. They genuinely thought that Muawiyah would soon realise the power of the state, and would respect and obey it.

On the other hand, Muawiyah and his followers believed that Imam Ali was merely testing their strength and their readiness. If he found them strong and well equipped, he would seek reconciliation through other means. Yet, the matter developed in a strange and unusual way. That sudden development points to the hidden forces who were at work in each camp to turn the dispute into full scale warfare.

Let us now conclude our discussion about this incident. As you may recall, Az-Zubair (may Allah be pleased with him) was fighting in the ranks of Muawiyah, but at the end of the battle he realised his mistake in joining the war altogether, and so he withdrew. However, some fighters followed him and stabbed him to death while he was praying. The killer amongst them robbed Az-Zubair of his sword and ran to Imam Ali, desiring to tell him the good news of the murder of Az-Zubair and to lay in his hands the sword he had used in fighting for Muawiyah against Ali. He came to the Imam's door asking for permission to enter. When Ali learned of the matter he shouted his command to dismiss the killer, saying, "Give the good tidings to the killer of Ibn Sufiyah that he will be cast in hellfire." By Ibn Sufiyah, he meant Az-Zubair (may Allah be pleased with him). He ordered further to have Az-Zubair's sword taken from the killer and brought to him.

When Ali saw the sword, he kept kissing it. He was crying and saying, "A sword whose owner had so many times removed the distress from the Messenger of Allah."

This remarkable scene bestows a strange kind of tranquillity upon the painful disagreement between Ali and Muawiyah. It fills us with much understanding and appreciation of the Companions as they truly were when we remember it.

———·◊·———

Now, we bid farewell to those men with whom we have travelled in the pages of this book. We thank Allah for His blessings, hoping to have more blessing, compassion, and good health from the Almighty.

With awe and reverence, we say to our eminent teacher, the last of the Messengers, "May the peace and mercy of Allah and His blessings be upon you. May Allah grant you the best reward for the teachings you gave and for your guidance." And with a renewed appreciation, we say to his blessed Companions, "Peace, Righteous Companions". It is a peace we extended at the start of this journey with awe and reverence; and it is a peace that remains in that awe and reverence, as we draw to a close.

www.ingramcontent.com/pod-product-compliance
Lightning Source LLC
Chambersburg PA
CBHW011316080526
44588CB00020B/2729